PRACTICING SCIENCE

The Investigative Approach in College Science Teaching

AN NSTA PRESS
JOURNALS COLLECTION

NATIONAL SCIENCE TEACHERS ASSOCIATION

NATIONAL SCIENCE TEACHERS ASSOCIATION

Shirley Watt Ireton, Director
Beth Daniels, Managing Editor
Judy Cusick, Associate Editor
Jessica Green, Assistant Editor
Linda Olliver, Cover Design

Art and Design
Linda Olliver, Director
NSTA Web
Tim Weber, Webmaster
Periodicals Publishing
Shelley Carey, Director
Printing and Production
Catherine Lorrain-Hale, Director
Publications Operations
Erin Miller, Manager
*sci*LINKS
Tyson Brown, Manager

National Science Teachers Association
Gerald F. Wheeler, Executive Director
David Beacom, Publisher

NSTA Press, NSTA Journals, and the NSTA Website deliver high-quality resources for science educators.

Practicing Science: The Investigative Approach in College Science Teaching
NSTA Stock Number: PB157X
ISBN 0-87355-195-8
Library of Congress Control Number: 2001087925
Printed in the USA by IPC Communications, Inc.
Printed on recycled paper

Contents

Acknowledgments iv

Introduction v

What Should Students Learn about the Nature of Science and How Should
We Teach It? Applying the "If-And-Then-Therefore" Pattern to Develop
Students' Theoretical Reasoning Abilities in Science 1
Anton E. Lawson (May 1999)

A Science-in-the-Making Course for Nonscience Majors: Reinforcing the
Scientific Method Using an Inquiry Approach 12
Deborah A. Tolman (September/October 1999)

Investigative Learning in Undergraduate Freshman Biology Laboratories:
A Pilot Project at Virginia Tech—New Roles for Students and Teachers in an Experimental
Design Laboratory 18
George E. Glasson and Woodrow L. McKenzie (December 1997/January 1998)

Use of an Investigative Semester-Length Laboratory Project in an Introductory Microbiology
Course: Acquainting Students with the Research Process and the Scientific Frame of Mind 23
Philip Stukus and John E. Lennox (November 1995)

Old Wine into New Bottles: How Traditional Lab Exercises Can Be Converted
into Investigative Ones 28
G. Douglas Crandall (May 1997)

Semester-Length Field Investigations in Undergraduate Animal Behavior and Ecology Courses:
Making the Laboratory Experience the Linchpin of Science Education 34
Jeffrey D. Weld, Christopher M. Rogers, and Stephen B. Heard (March/April 1999)

Full Application of the Scientific Method in an Undergraduate Teaching Laboratory:
A Reality-Based Approach to Experiential Student-Directed Instruction 39
Alan R. Harker (November 1999)

Student-Designed Physiology Laboratories: Creative Instructional Alternatives at a Resource-Poor
New England University 43
Linda L. Tichenor (December 1996/January 1997)

Problem-Based Learning in Physics: The Power of Students Teaching Students—
Discovering the Interplay between Science and Today's World 50
Barbara J. Duch (March/April 1996)

A Multidimensional Approach to Teaching Biology: Injecting Analytical Thought
into the Scientific Process 54
*Dwight D. Dimaculangan, Paula L. Mitchell, William Rogers, John M. Schmidt, Janice L. Chism, and
James W. Johnston* (March/April 2000)

Authors' Affiliations and Contact Information as of February 2001 61

Acknowledgments

The ten articles in *Practicing Science: The Investigative Approach in College Science Teaching* were selected from the *Journal of College Science Teaching* (1995-2001) by a committee of higher education science faculty. The committee was headed by William J. McIntosh, professor of science education at Delaware State University and director of the College Division of the National Science Teachers Association's (NSTA) Committee on College Science Teaching. Also on the committee were Mario Caprio, adjunct professor of biology, Volunteer State Community College; Michael Marlow, associate professor in the School of Education, University of Colorado; and Nannette Smith, director of the Division of Natural, Behavioral, and Social Sciences, Bennett College.

Judy Cusick was the NSTA project editor for the book. Claudia Link, managing editor of *The Journal of College Science Teaching*, provided invaluable assistance at each stage of the book's development. Linda Olliver designed the cover, Nguyet Tran handled book layout, and Catherine Lorrain-Hale coordinated production and printing.

Introduction

Practicing Science: The Investigative Approach in College Science Teaching describes how the skills and processes of investigative learning—inquiry—can be developed and nurtured in the college science classroom. To build this collection, reviewers chose articles from the *Journal of College Science Teaching* that show how college faculty have modified their classes and labs to provide more opportunities to develop inquiry skills. The selected articles illustrate how inquiry contributes to scientific literacy and why it should be a part of all college students' experiences.

The abilities of inquiry to which the *National Science Education Standards* (NRC 1996) refer need little elaboration for college science teachers, who most likely have designed and conducted their own scientific investigations. The Standards use the term to mean (a) a set of abilities and understandings and (b) a set of instructional strategies. Inquiry abilities include identifying researchable questions, designing and conducting scientific investigations, and using logic and evidence to support claims. Inquiry instructional strategies include providing experiences that require students to pose and respond to authentic questions that demand interpretation of evidence and problem solving.

The value of inquiry is described by Lawson in his article "What Should Students Learn about the Nature of Science and How Should We Teach It?" Lawson discusses, in the context of contemporary learning theory, an instructional approach that promotes sound scientific reasoning. His conclusions support inquiry as a means of developing thinking skills and learning about the nature of science.

In "A Science-in-the-Making Course for Nonscience Majors," Tolman describes how her nonmajors pose questions, analyze data, and generally carry out nontraditional activities as they engage in a series of projects designed to give them firsthand experiences with scientific inquiry.

Other articles in this book describe different degrees to which professors have infused inquiry into their courses. One approach is to substitute an inquiry investigation for part or all of an existing lab program. Glasson and McKenzie, in "Investigative Learning in Undergraduate Freshman Biology Laboratories," describe a lab approach whereby students are asked to collaboratively design a series of short-term experiments. Students, with help from teaching assistants, create hypotheses, test their ideas, and propose explanations.

As outlined in "Use of an Investigative Semester-Length Laboratory Project in an Introductory Microbiology Course," Stukus and Lennox require groups of students to conduct a culminating investigation to isolate a randomly selected microorganism. Students conduct library research, formulate their own isolation procedures, and present their results in a final paper. The professors take time at the beginning of the semester to build the student skills required for the investigation that follows. In this approach, lab experiences early in the semester lay the groundwork for those that follow.

Crandall, in "Old Wine into New Bottles: How Traditional Lab Exercises Can Be Converted into Investigative Ones," discusses his experiences with converting traditional labs into investigative ones. He too takes a developmental approach that begins with a discussion early in the semester that weaves together content and experimental design. Crandall follows this discussion with a guided investigation designed to orient students to data collection procedures and interpretation skills. Students then begin to design their own experiments.

Some professors, like Weld, Rogers, and Heard, have their students conduct semester-length laboratory investigations. As they discuss in "Semester-Length Field Investigations in Undergraduate Animal Behavior and Ecology Courses," student teams spend twenty-five to forty hours in the field conducting authentic research that requires them to create hypotheses, make predictions, and design and carry out their own investigations.

Similarly, Harker's students, as described in "Full Application of the Scientific Method in an Undergraduate Teaching Laboratory," select a topic in the beginning of the semester and pursue it in small groups with little teacher intervention. Each group is entirely responsible for its own project and often meets outside of scheduled lab time.

Tichenor, as outlined in "Student-Designed Physiology Laboratories," takes a different approach. She has students work collaboratively during the semester to develop inquiry-based labs that are performed later in the semester by other students in the class. Her incremental, phased approach prepares students to design and carry out their own lab exercises. Students evaluate each other's experiments for content and design flaws.

Students in Duch's physics course, as described in "Problem-Based Learning in Physics," learn to see the world from a different point of view. Throughout the semester, they take the role of, for example, a health care worker or an accident investigator to engage in real world problem solving. Like the other contributors to this book, Duch uses field trips, research projects, and cooperative problem solving experiences to challenge students' inquiry skills.

A larger-scale approach to inquiry teaching and learning is illustrated when entire courses are completely revised to encourage more student inquiry. In "A Multidimensional Approach to Teaching Biology," Dimaculangan, Mitchell, Rogers, Schmidt, Chism, and Johnson describe three courses in which students build knowledge and skills throughout the semester as they move from mini-investigations to independent projects.

In summary, the professors featured in this compendium have revised their labs—and, in some cases, their entire courses—so their students have multiple opportunities to develop the abilities and understandings of inquiry. They supplement the traditional lecture with instructional strategies shown to be more effective in meeting inquiry goals. Their successful efforts serve as examples for those who wish to do the same.

Reference
National Research Council (NRC). 1996. *The National Science Education Standards.* Washington DC: National Academy Press.

What Should Students Learn About the Nature of Science and How Should We Teach It?

Applying the "If-And-Then-Therefore" Pattern to Develop Students' Theoretical Reasoning Abilities in Science

Anton E. Lawson

This article attempts to: 1) explicate the basic pattern of scientific reasoning, 2) show how the pattern has been used to answer a wide range of scientific questions, and 3) argue that sequencing instruction that focuses on that reasoning pattern first in observable contexts and then in non-observable contexts helps students better understand the nature of science and use scientific reasoning in and beyond the science classroom.

Teaching in ways that help students understand the nature of science and how to use scientific reasoning patterns have long been central goals of science education (American Association for the Advancement of Science [AAAS] 1928, 1989, 1990; Educational Policies Commission 1961, 1966; National Science Foundation 1996; National Research Council 1995; National Society for the Study of Education 1960).

However, in spite of a general and long-term philosophical commitment to these goals, the vast majority of research forces the conclusion that the goals have been largely unfulfilled (Lederman 1992; MacKay 1971; National Assessment of Educational Progress 1988; Ryan and Aikenhead 1992).

Part of the problem can be attributed to a justifiable confusion about just what the nature of science is and just what constitutes effective patterns of scientific reasoning. This problem was stated nicely some time ago by the Nobel Prize winning physicist Richard Feynman in an address at the 1966 annual convention of the National Science Teachers Association (Feynman 1966).

In response to the question, What is science?, Feynman was reminded of the following poem: "A centipede was quite happy until a toad in fun said, Pray, which leg comes after which? This raised his doubts to such a pitch, He fell distracted in a ditch."

Feynman went on to remark, "All my life I have been doing science and known what it was, but what I have come to tell you—which foot comes after which—I am unable to do, and furthermore, I am worried by the analogy with the poem, that when I go home, I will no longer be able to do any research."

In spite of Feynman's reservations about how to describe the nature of science, the purpose of this article is to: 1) explicate the central pattern of scientific reasoning, 2) show that the pattern has been applied by scientists to help answer a wide range of scientific questions, and 3) argue that sequencing instruction that focuses on that reasoning pattern first in observable and familiar contexts and then in non-observable and unfamiliar contexts will help students not only better understand what science is, but also help them successfully apply scientific reasoning patterns in and beyond the science classroom.

HOW DO PEOPLE LEARN?

Take a few minutes to try the task presented in **Figure 1**. You will need a mirror. Once you have a mirror, place the figure down in front of it so that you can look into the mirror at the reflected figure. Read and follow

Anton E. Lawson is a professor in the department of biology, Arizona State University, Tempe, AZ 85287-1501; e-mail: anton.lawson@asu.edu.

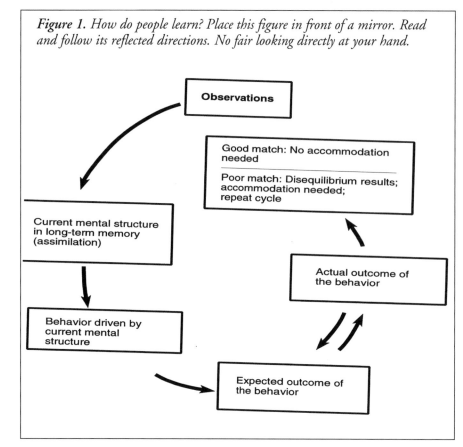

Figure 1. How do people learn? Place this figure in front of a mirror. Read and follow its reflected directions. No fair looking directly at your hand.

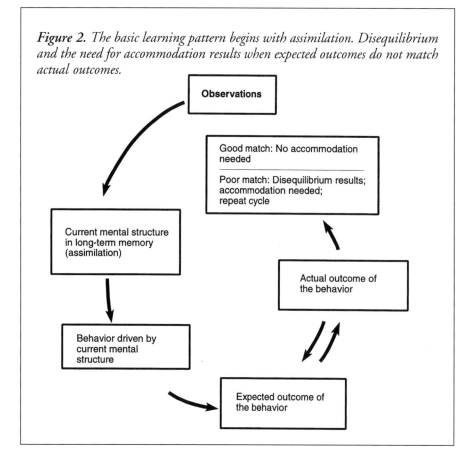

Figure 2. The basic learning pattern begins with assimilation. Disequilibrium and the need for accommodation results when expected outcomes do not match actual outcomes.

the figure's reflected directions. Look only in the mirror—no fair peeking directly at your hand. When finished, read on.

How did you do? If you are like most people, the task proved rather difficult and frustrating. Of course, this should come as no surprise. After all, you have spent a lifetime writing and drawing without a mirror. So what does this little mirror-drawing task tell us about how people learn and about the nature of science?

I think it reveals the basic learning pattern depicted in **Figure 2** and described as follows: First, the reflected images are assimilated by specific "mental structures" that are currently part of your long-term memory. These mental structures then drive behavior that, in the past, has been linked to consequences (i.e., actual outcomes). Thus, when the structures are used to drive behavior in the present context, the behavior is linked to an expected outcome.

All is well if the behavior is successful—that is, if its actual outcome matches the expected outcome. However, if unsuccessful, that is, if its actual outcome does not match the expected one (e.g., your hand moves to the left and down and you expect to see a line drawn to the left and down, but instead you see one drawn to the left and *up*), contradiction results.

This contradiction then drives a subconscious search for another mental structure and perhaps a closer inspection of the figure until either another structure is found that works (in the sense that it drives successful, noncontradicted behavior), or you become so frustrated that you quit. In the latter case, your mental structures will not undergo the necessary accommodation (cf. Karplus, Lawson, Wollman, Appel, Bernoff, Howe, Rusch, and Sullivan 1977; Piaget 1971; Lawson 1994). In other words, you won't learn to draw successfully in a mirror.

CAN THIS LEARNING PATTERN BE USED TO ANSWER "SCIENTIFIC" QUESTIONS?

The top row of **Figure 3** shows

"creatures" called Mellinarks. Notice that none of the creatures in the second row are Mellinarks. Your job in this task is to figure out which creatures in the third row are Mellinarks. Take a few minutes to see what you come up with.

Did you conclude that creatures one, two, and six of row three are Mellinarks? If so, how did you arrive at that conclusion? This question is tough because it is difficult to reflect on one's reasoning. Nevertheless, allow me to present a strategy that previous research indicates successful students use (Lawson 1993). See if it comes close to what you did. First, we glance at the Mellinarks in the first row and see that they all contain one large dot. Could one large dot be the key feature of Mellinarks? We can test this idea as follows:

If...Mellinarks are creatures with one large dot (proposed key feature),
and...we look at the non-Mellinarks in row two (behavioral test),
then...none of them should contain a large dot (expected outcome).
But...creatures one, two, and four in row two each contain a large dot (actual outcome).
Therefore...Mellinarks are not creatures defined solely by the presence of one large dot. We need to generate and test another idea (conclusion).

Recycling this reasoning pattern eventually prompts the reasoner to generate, test, and support the idea that Mellinarks are defined by the presence of one large dot, a curly tail, and shading. Hence, creatures one, two, and six in row three are Mellinarks. Notice in **Figure 4** that this if-and-then-therefore pattern is the same pattern used in the mirror task. The primary difference is that the mirror task was nonverbal and sensory-motor, while the Mellinark task involves feature detection and linguistically-mediated arguments to arrive at a successful (i.e., noncontradicted) classification scheme of Mellinarks and non-Mellinarks.

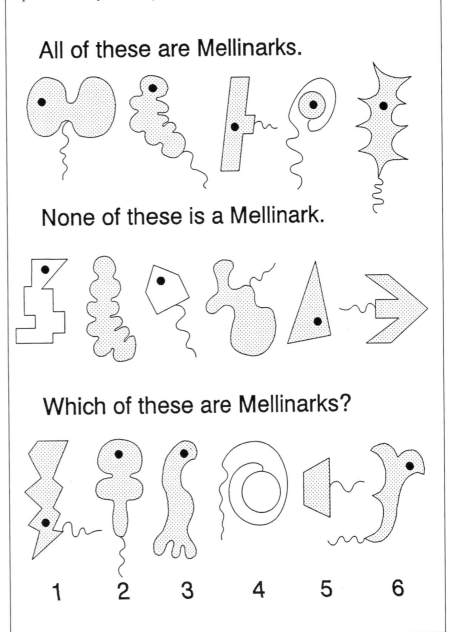

Figure 3. Which creatures in row three are Mellinarks? What reasoning pattern(s) did you use to find out?

All of these are Mellinarks.

None of these is a Mellinark.

Which of these are Mellinarks?

1 2 3 4 5 6

CAN THE SAME REASONING PATTERN BE USED IN CAUSAL CONTEXTS?

Successfully identifying features and variables, and using them to form classes and subclasses of objects, is an important component of science. But there is much more to science than description and classification. Scientists seek to understand nature in terms of causes and effects. Can the if-and-then-therefore pattern also be used in causal contexts?

Consider the case of silver salmon. Silver salmon are found in the headwaters of freshwater streams in the Pacific Northwest. Young salmon swim downstream to the Pacific Ocean, where they grow and mature sexually. They then return to the freshwater streams and swim upstream to ultimately lay their eggs in the headwaters before dying. By tagging young salmon, biologists discovered that mature salmon actually migrate to precisely the same headwaters in which they hatched some years earlier. This discovery raised a very interesting question: How do returning salmon locate their homestreams?

A number of alternative hypotheses can be proposed. For instance, humans often navigate by sight. Perhaps salmon do as well. Salmon may remember certain objects, such as large rocks they saw when swimming downstream on their way to the ocean. They then see these and use them to navigate on their return journey.

Studies of migratory animals also suggest hypotheses. For example, biologists have found that migratory eels are enormously sensitive to dissolved minerals. Perhaps salmon are as well. In other words, perhaps salmon use their noses to detect smells specific to their homestreams.

Thus, the use of analogies (i.e., borrowing ideas from similar contexts—sometimes referred to as analogical reasoning) gives us two alternative hypotheses: Salmon use sight to find their homestream. Or salmon smell substances specific to their homestream, which they follow upstream.

The next task is to test the alternatives. During the 1960s, American biologist A.D. Hasler conducted an experiment to test the sight hypothesis using the following reasoning:

*If...*silver salmon locate their homestream by sight (sight hypothesis),

*and...*returning salmon are captured from two homestreams (see **Figure 5**). Some fish from each stream are then blindfolded, while others are not. All of the fish are then released below the junction where the streams join, and the returning fish are then recaptured in traps above the junction as they swim back up the streams (test conditions),

*then...*the blindfolded salmon should be recaptured in their homestreams at a significantly lower rate than the non-blindfolded salmon (expected result).

*But...*the blindfolded salmon were recaptured in their homestreams at the

Figure 4. The basic learning pattern applied to the Mellinark task.

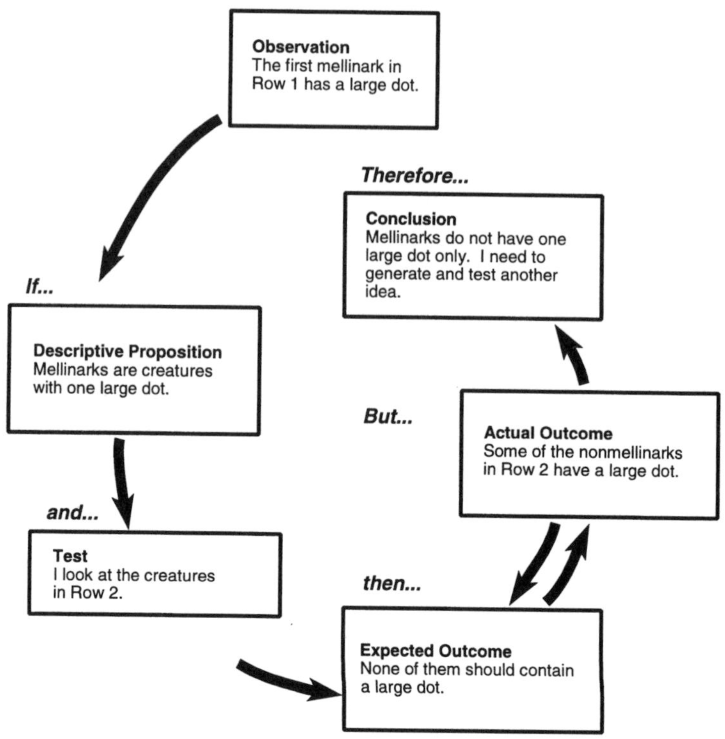

same rate as the non-blindfolded salmon (actual result).

*Therefore...*the sight hypothesis is contradicted (conclusion).

This example shows that the if-and-then-therefore reasoning pattern can indeed be used to test causal hypotheses. Importantly, in spite of the similarity in pattern, students as young as seven years old can successfully use if-and-then-therefore reasoning to solve Mellinark-type tasks—that is to solve descriptive/classification tasks (Lawson 1993). But they do not successfully apply it to test hypotheses in causal contexts until much later—around age 12 (Inhelder and Piaget 1958). In fact some college-age students still exhibit difficulties in its use in causal contexts—a point that will be returned to later (Dawson and Rowell 1986; Lawson 1992; Walker 1979).

Before leaving the salmon example, one further point should be made. (By the way, Hasler did eventually find support for the smell hypothesis as fish

with their noses plugged were not as good at finding their homestreams as those that could smell.) Consider the relationship between Hasler's sight and smell hypotheses and the independent variables manipulated in his experiments. In effect, the possible causes—the hypotheses—were the manipulated variables, i.e., the ability-to-see variable and the ability-to-smell variable.

In other words, to experimentally test these types of causal hypotheses, you manipulate the hypothesized cause (i.e., you blindfold the fish, you plug the fishes' noses), and you wait to see if the outcome is affected (i.e., the fish stop returning to their homestream). If the outcome is affected, then the hypothesis is supported. If not, the hypothesis is contradicted; something else is probably causing the effect.

IS IF-AND-THEN-THEREFORE REASONING ALSO USED IN CORRELATIONAL CONTEXTS?

But one can not always manipulate hypothesized causes. Sometimes correlational evidence is all that one can obtain. Can if-and-then-therefore reasoning also be used to test hypotheses with correlational data? Suppose one wants to test the hypothesis that silicone-gel-filled breast implants cause connective-tissue disease in women. Clearly experimentation is unethical and out of the question. Nevertheless, consider the following argument:

If...silicone-gel-filled breast implants cause connective-tissue disease (breast-implants-cause-disease hypothesis)

and...the incidence of connective tissue disease in women with silicone-gel implants is compared with disease incidence in women without implants (test conditions)

then...the disease incidence should be significantly higher for the women with implants than for those without implants (expected results).

But...the disease incidence is not significantly higher for women with implants. For example, a 1994 study reported in *The New England Journal of Medicine* found a 0.06% incidence of connective-tissue disease among women with implants. Disease incidence among an age-matched group of women without implants from the same area for the same time period was

also 0.06% (actual results).

Therefore...the breast-implants-cause-connective-tissue-disease hypothesis is contradicted (conclusion).

Notice that the preceding argument and correlational evidence do indeed test the causal hypothesis, though not as convincingly as a controlled experiment might. Can if-and-then-therefore reasoning also be used to test scientific theories that claim the existence of unseen entities?

HOW ARE THEORIES THAT CLAIM THE EXISTENCE OF UNSEEN ENTITIES TESTED?

The ancient Greeks discovered that a candle placed under an inverted jar burns for a short time and then goes out. By the 1700s most scientists explained this by imagining that materials, such as candles, consist of a base plus something called phlogiston. According to phlogiston theory, when a candle burns, its unseen phlogiston is released into the air and its base is left behind as ashes. Thus, a flame under the inverted jar goes out because the jar's air becomes saturated with phlogiston. When the air is full of phlogiston, burning stops and the flame goes out.

Phlogiston theory makes sense and it seems to agree with the observations. Certainly one can "observe" flames going from candles into air. But phlogiston theory was not entirely free of difficulties as can be seen in the following argument:

If...phlogiston is an unseen material (which like other materials has weight) that escapes from metals during burning (phlogiston theory)

and...a metal is weighed before and after it burns and turns into ashes (test condition),

then...the ashes should weigh less than the original metal (expected result). The ashes should weigh less because part of the initial material (the phlogiston) has escaped into the air (theoretical rationale).

But...the ashes weigh more, not less, than the original metal (observed result).

Therefore...phlogiston theory is contradicted (conclusion).

What do you suppose the phlogistonists did with this contradictory result? Instead of rejecting the theory, they simply imagined that phlogiston has *negative* weight! Consequently, they argued that adding phlogiston to something should decrease its weight, and removing phlogiston should increase its weight.

The idea of negative weight may seem much too strange to take seriously. But it does make some sense. After all, phlogistonists argued, fire seeks its "natural" place above air, thus, fire (phlogiston) should have negative weight. If you still think this idea of negative weight is too strange, consider the "attractive" *and* "repulsive" forces of common magnets, forces that were well known at the time. If magnets can attract *and* repel things, why can't phlogiston have negative weight? Small wonder that phlogiston theory was well accepted by eighteenth-century chemists.

Regardless of the fact that contradictory results do not necessarily cause people to abandon theories, the phlogiston example does at least

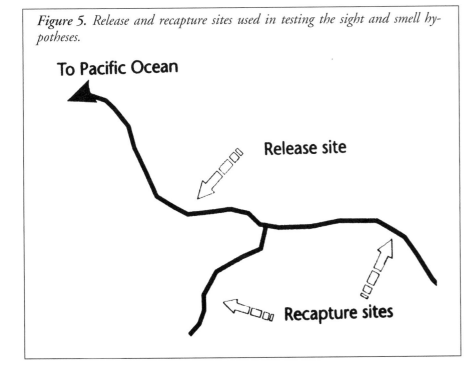

Figure 5. Release and recapture sites used in testing the sight and smell hypotheses.

To Pacific Ocean

Release site

Recapture sites

demonstrate that if-and-then-therefore reasoning can be used to put theories about unseen entities to the test. Let's consider one more example.

HOW DO NERVE IMPULSES PASS BETWEEN CELLS?

A microscopic look at the place where one neuron contacts another, or where a neuron contacts a muscle cell, reveals that the cells come very close to one another, but they do not touch. Instead, tiny gaps called synapses exist. In other words, synapses separate neurons from each other and from muscle cells. Thus, another question presents itself: How do nerve impulses travel across synapses?

During the late 1800s and early 1900s, most physiologists suspected that electrical transmission was involved. Diffusing chemicals just seemed too slow to account for the apparent speed of transmission. Nevertheless, in 1921, chemical-transmission theory got a big boost thanks to a most improbable experiment conducted by German physiologist Otto Loewi.

Loewi's experiment involved a frog whose heart he dissected out along with the nerve connecting the heart to the spinal cord. When Loewi electrically stimulated the nerve, the heartbeat slowed. So apparently the nerve helps regulate heart rate. Loewi then thought of a way to use the nerve and heart to test chemical-transmission theory. In fact, he thought of the test in a dream! He was so excited by his dream that he awoke and immediately wrote down his plan. But in the morning when he tried to read what he had written, he found it unintelligible. Fortunately, a few nights later, the dream recurred.

This time, taking no chances, Loewi awoke and immediately went to his lab to conduct the test. His reasoning and test went as follows:

*If...*the transmission of impulses between neurons and from neurons to muscle cells involves the flow of molecules across synapses (chemical-transmission theory)

*and...*the frog's nerve (mentioned above) is stimulated several times to slow its heart rate while the heart is bathed in a fluid (test conditions),

*then...*when that fluid is collected and applied to another frog's heart, its heartbeat should also slow (expected result). This result is expected because the imagined molecules produced by the stimulated nerve in the nerve-heart preparation should pass through the synapses separating the neurons and heart muscle cells and collect in the fluid. So when the fluid is applied to the second heart, the molecules in the fluid should produce the same effect, that is slow the second heart (theoretical rationale).

*And...*as expected, Loewi found that the fluid caused the second heart to slow. The fluid had the same effect on several other tissues as well (actual result).

*Therefore...*Loewi's improbable experiment provided convincing support for chemical-transmission theory (conclusion). The unseen diffusing chemical was later identified as acetylcholine.

HOW GOOD ARE COLLEGE STUDENTS AT GENERATING THEORETICAL ARGUMENTS?

College students are fairly proficient at generating if-and-then-therefore arguments in contexts in which the hypothesized causes are observable and relatively familiar (e.g., salmon experiment, breast-implant situation). But doing the same in theoretical contexts that involve unseen entities such as phlogiston or acetylcholine proves much more difficult.

More specifically, following instruction, over 90 percent of the college students in a recent study successfully generated if-and-then-therefore arguments when the proposed causes were familiar and observable. But less than 25 percent did so when they were unfamiliar and unseen (Lawson, Drake, Johnson, Kwon, and Scarpone 1997). Why should this be?

The answer may in part be simply due to lack of familiarity and the fact that the proposed causal agents are no longer observable. But there may be more to it than this. Notice that testing ideas in theoretical contexts also requires an extra step in reasoning. Whereas the previous experimental or correlational tests directly manipulated or varied the hypothesized causes, this is no longer the case in theoretical contexts.

For example, in the phlogiston test, the proposed cause of flames going out was the saturation of air with an unseen substance (phlogiston) and the experiment involved weighing a metal before and after burning. Similarly, in Loewi's experiment, the imagined cause of impulse transmission was the diffusion of unseen molecules across synapses, and the experiment involved the stimulation of frog's nerve while its connected heart was bathed in fluid, and then placing that fluid on a second heart.

In other words, the relationship between the proposed cause and the experimental design is no longer obvious and direct. Consequently, a theoretical rationale (i.e., an explicit statement of the relationship between the imagined cause and the test) needs to be added to the argument.

HOW CAN TEACHERS HELP STUDENTS DEVELOP THEORETICAL REASONING PATTERNS?

As we have seen, learning involves an idea-testing process that follows the if-and-then-therefore pattern. The pattern may be explicitly stated, as was the case for several scientific examples in this paper; or it may operate on a subconscious, nonverbal level, as was the case for the mirror drawing. Moreover, the development of scientific reasoning patterns (i.e., acquisition of learning-to-learn strategies) appears to occur in a sequential stage-like manner in which the if-and-then-therefore pattern is first applied in sensory-motor contexts and only later in descriptive (i.e., categorical) Mellinark-like contexts, and still later in hypothetical contexts. Some people, including scientists, even develop the ability to use the pattern in theoretical contexts.

Importantly, it would seem that development of this sort of theoretical reasoning ability is necessary for understanding the theoretical nature of science. Given that few college students give evidence of theoretical reasoning ability (perhaps less than 25 percent), the key pedagogical question is this: How can we help the other 75 percent develop theoretical reasoning patterns and acquire an accurate understanding of the nature of science?

If intellectual development is truly stage-like, then for "descriptive" students it would appear that we need to immerse them in "hypothetical" contexts and provide lots of opportunities for direct physical experience, for social interaction with others, and for equilibration (cf., Piaget and Inhelder 1969). Once these students develop hypothetical reasoning patterns, we then need to repeat the process in theoretical contexts.

In other words, as teachers we need to: 1) know where our students are in their intellectual development, 2) be aware of the intellectual demands that instructional tasks place on student reasoning abilities, 3) correctly match instructional contexts with student abilities, and 4) sequence contexts in a way that moves from description and classification, to causal hypothesis testing in familiar contexts, to causal hypothesis testing in not-so-familiar contexts, and then to theory testing (where theories are defined as general explanatory systems that postulate the existence of unseen entities and/or processes).

WHY DOES WATER RISE IN THE CYLINDER?

Let's see how we can teach a lesson involving use of if-and-then-therefore thinking and unseen theoretical entities to help students develop theoretical reasoning patterns and a more accurate understanding of the nature of science.

Background Information. The lesson begins with a burning candle held upright in a pan of water using a small piece of clay. Shortly after a cylinder is inverted over the burning candle and placed in the water, the candle flame goes out and water rises in the cylinder. These observations raise two ma-

---

Table 1. Postulates of Kinetic-Molecular Theory Used to Explain the Water Rise.

1. *The universe contains matter, which is composed of tiny particles (atoms and combinations of atoms called molecules) and light, which consists of still smaller particles called photons.*

2. *Atoms/molecules are in constant motion. They strike other atoms/molecules and transfer some or all of their motion (kinetic energy) to these particles.*

3. *An energy source, such as a flame, consists of rapidly moving particles that can transfer some, or all, of their motion to nearby particles through collisions.*

4. *Attractive forces between atoms or molecules can be broken, causing the atoms or molecules to move apart, which in turn can cause collisions and transfers of energy (motion).*

5. *Molecular bonds can form between atoms when they strike one another.*

6. *Temperature is a measure of the amount of motion (average kinetic energy) of the atoms/molecules in a solid, liquid, or gas (i.e., the more motion the greater the temperature).*

7. *Air pressure is a force exerted on a surface due to collisions of air particles (i.e., more particles at higher velocities = greater air pressure).*

---

jor causal questions: Why did the flame go out? And why did the water rise?

The generally accepted answer to the first question is that the flame converted the oxygen in the cylinder to carbon dioxide such that too little oxygen remained to sustain combustion, thus the flame died. The generally accepted answer to the second question is that the flame transfers kinetic energy (motion) to the cylinder's gas molecules. The greater kinetic energy causes the gas to expand, which results in some escaping out the bottom. When the flame goes out, the remaining molecules transfer some of their kinetic energy to the cylinder walls and then to the surrounding air and water.

This transfer causes a loss of average velocity, fewer collisions, and less gas pressure (a partial vacuum). This partial vacuum is then filled by water rising into the cylinder until the air pressure pushing on the outside water surface is equal to the air pressure pushing on the inside surface (Peckham 1993).

This lesson is a particularly good way to reinforce the idea that science is an alternative explanation, generation, and testing enterprise as the initial explanations students often generate to explain why the water rises are experimentally contradicted. Hence, mental disequilibrium results along with the need for accommodation. In other words, their ideas need to be replaced.

A common student explanation centers around the idea that oxygen is "used up," thus a partial vacuum is created, which "sucks" water into the cylinder. Typically, students fail to realize that when oxygen "burns" it combines with carbon producing CO_2 gas of equal volume (hence no partial vacuum is created). Students also often fail to realize that a vacuum cannot "suck" anything. Rather the force causing the water to rise is a push from the relatively greater number of air molecules hitting the water surface outside the cylinder.

Student experiments and discussions provide an opportunity to modify these misconceptions by introducing a more satisfactory explanation of combustion and air pressure. An opportunity also exists to portray science as an intellectually stimulating and challenging way of using theories, in this case kinetic-molecular theory (see **Table 1**) to explain nature.

Starting the Lesson. Start the lesson by pointing out the following

materials:
- ▲ aluminum pie pans
- ▲ birthday candles
- ▲ matches
- ▲ modeling clay
- ▲ cylinders (open at one end)
- ▲ jars (of various shapes, sizes)
- ▲ beakers and/test tubes/flasks
- ▲ syringes and rubber tubing
- ▲ baking soda
- ▲ ice
- ▲ dry ice
- ▲ balloons
- ▲ pH paper

Have each student select a partner. Tell each pair to pour some water into the pan. Stand a candle in the pan using a small piece of clay for support. Then light the candle and put a cylinder, jar, flask, or beaker over the candle so that it covers the candle and sits in the water. Then observe what happens and repeat the procedure several times varying several independent variables (e.g., the number of candles, amount of water, type of cylinder) to determine their possible effects.

You should also tell students that they will not only be challenged to generate several alternative explanations for what they observe, but they will also be challenged to design experiments to test the alternatives. (Of particular interest is the fact that on a number of past occasions "hypothetical" students—and sometimes teachers—feel that they have completed the lesson when they have identified variables that affect the level of water rise. They don't even realize that their "theoretical" task has just begun!)

Generating Alternative Explanations. Allow the initial exploration to proceed as long as students are making good progress. You may need to stop them after about 30-40 minutes to discuss observations, preliminary questions, and explanations. During the discussion, observations should be listed on the board and you should ask students to state the key causal question(s) raised.

The most obvious causal questions are: Why did the flame go out? And why did the water rise? Alternative explanations that students may generate

to answer the second question include:

1) The oxygen is "burned up" creating a partial vacuum. So the water is "sucked" in to replace it.

2) H_2O gas is formed by burning. When the H_2O cools, it changes to liquid filling the cylinder.

3) As the candle burns, it consumes O_2 but produces an equal volume of CO_2. The CO_2 dissolves in the water more easily than the original O_2, producing a partial vacuum. The water is then "sucked" in.

4) The candle produces smoke, which collects in the cylinder and attracts (pulls) the water up.

5) Burning converts O_2 to CO_2, which is a smaller molecule. Thus, it takes up less space, creating a partial vacuum that "sucks" the water up.

6) The candle's heat causes the air around it to expand. After the candle goes out, the air cools, air pressure is reduced, and the water is pushed in by greater air pressure outside. (If no one proposes this explanation you will have to propose it yourself. But make sure that you do not give students the impression that this is the "correct" explanation. Rather, it is simply an idea that a student in another class generated, which should be tested along with the others.)

7) Here is an explanation that I like to add to the students' list: A Wizard named Sparky lives on campus and sucks the water up. (Sparky is the name of our university sports mascot).

Testing the Alternatives. Now that student brainstorming has generated several possible explanations, remind students that this is a science class.

Consequently, their next task is to test the alternatives. Also remind them that to test a possible explanation one must conduct experiments with clearly stated expected results (predictions).

You may want to provide an example, or simply challenge students to put their heads together to see what they can come up with. This may be an excellent time for the bell to ring so that they can think up experiments as a homework assignment. If you do decide to offer an example, use the if-and-then-therefore form. For example:

If...explanation 1 is correct, that is if water is "sucked" up because oxygen is consumed creating a partial vacuum (oxygen-consumed explanation)

The history of science has much to offer to help us identify "natural" routes of inquiry, routes that past scientists have taken and routes that present students can also take—routes that should lead to scientific literacy. That is, to students who know what science is and how to do it.

---

and...the height that water rises with one, two , three, or more candles (all other things being equal) is measured (test conditions)

then...the height of water rise should be the same regardless of the number of burning candles (expected result). This result is expected presumably because there is only so much oxygen in the cylinder to be burned. So more candles will burn up the available oxygen faster than fewer candles, but they will not burn up more oxygen. Hence, the water level should rise the same. Note that the assumption is made that before they go out, more candles do not consume more oxygen than fewer candles (theoretical rationale).

Now have students conduct their experiments and report results. Results of the example experiment show that the water level is affected by the number of candles (the more candles the higher the water level). Therefore the oxygen-consumed explanation has been contradicted. Also the water rises after the candles go out, not while they are burning—another observation that contradicts explanation 1.

Explanation 2, the water-created-by-burning explanation, can be tested by measuring the total volume of water before and after the water has risen inside. If this explanation is correct, the total volume of water should increase considerably.

Explanation 3 claims that the CO_2 dissolves in the water. Students can test this explanation in a couple of ways. One way involves a comparison of the amount of water rise in containers with CO_2-saturated water versus normal water. The explanation leads to the prediction that the water level should rise higher in the cylinder with normal water. One can use dry ice (or sodium bicarbonate and acid) to produce CO_2 gas. Its solubility in water can be tested. The pH of water shaken with CO_2 and the pH of the water below a candle that has just gone out can be compared.

Also, if the explanation is correct, a cylinder filled with gas from the dry ice (presumably CO_2) when inverted and placed in water should cause water to rise, but water doesn't.

Explanation 4, the smoke-attracts-water explanation, can be tested by filling a cylinder with smoke and inverting it in water. If the explanation is correct, the water should rise.

I will leave it to you to figure out a way to test explanation 5, the CO_2-is-a-smaller-molecule explanation.

Explanation 6, the heat-causes-air-expansion explanation, leads to the prediction that bubbles should be seen escaping out the bottom of the cylinder (assuming that the cylinder is quickly placed over the candles while the air is still expanding). It also leads to the prediction that more candles should cause more water to rise—presumably because more candles will heat more air, thus, more will escape, which in turn will be replaced by more water. (Although one candle burning over a longer time period releases as much energy as three candles burning a shorter time, one candle will not raise the cylinder's air temperature as much because energy is dissipated rather quickly.)

Initially students do not take explanation 7, the Sparky-sucks explanation, seriously. So they don't bother to test it. But at my insistence, they soon come up with the idea of conducting the experiment off campus based on the following reasoning:

*If...*the water rises because Sparky sucks it up (Sparky explanation)
*and...*the experiment is conducted off campus (test condition)
*then...*the water should not rise (expected result).
*But...*they surmise that the water does rise off campus (actual result).
*Therefore...*the Sparky explanation can be rejected (conclusion).

I reply to this argument that, since they are Arizona State University students, Sparky travels with them off campus. Consequently, he can still make the water rise. So their experiment does not really contradict the Sparky explanation after all.

Students then propose to have the experiment done by telephoning a non-ASU student and asking him or her to conduct the experiment off campus. Then when the non-ASU student finds that the water still rises, students conclude that the Sparky explanation can be rejected. But Sparky's powers can travel through phone lines, I tell them, so the water should still rise.

At this point most students catch on to the game being played, which essentially amounts to giving Sparky ever-expanding powers. And once Sparky's powers become limitless, the Sparky explanation can no longer be tested. Thus, continued belief in Sparky becomes a matter of faith, not evidence. In other words, Sparky becomes a religious, God-like, entity, not a scientific (i.e., testable) entity. This discussion is important because it clarifies this essential difference between religion and science for many students for the first time.

Introducing and Applying Kinetic-Molecular Theory. After all the alternatives have been tested and the results discussed, you should carefully summarize and clarify the explanation that is most consistent with the evidence. You can also introduce the term air pressure and the major postulates of the kinetic-molecular theory as they pertain to the present phenomenon. You should also discuss the common misconception of "suction" in this context. Kinetic-molecular theory implies that suction (as a force that can suck up water) does not exist (i.e., the water is being pushed into the cylinder by moving particles of air rather than being sucked by some intuitively generated but nonexistent force).

To allow students to apply kinetic-molecular theory and the concept of air pressure to a new situation, provide each group a piece of rubber tubing, a syringe, a beaker, and a pan of water. Instruct them to invert the beaker in the pan of water and fill it with water in that position with the mouth of the beaker submerged. Some students will make futile efforts to force water through the tube into the beaker before discovering that they must extract the air through the tube.

As a homework assignment, challenge the students to find a way to insert a peeled, hard-boiled egg into a bottle with an opening that is smaller in diameter than the egg. They must not touch the egg with anything after it has been placed on the opening. After a small amount of water in the bottle has been heated, it is only necessary to place the smaller end of the egg over the opening of the bottle to form a seal. The egg will be forced into the bottle by the greater air pressure outside as the air inside cools. You may also ask students to drink a milk shake with a straw and then challenge them to explain how the milk shake gets into their mouths.

WHAT DOES THE CANDLE-BURNING LESSON TEACH STUDENTS ABOUT THE NATURE OF SCIENCE?

In addition to providing students with experience in using theoretical reasoning to generate and test alternative explanations, the candle-burning lesson exemplifies these important characteristics of science:

▲ Science is a human activity that attempts to accurately describe and explain nature by raising and answering descriptive and causal questions. Science consists of methods of description and explanation plus the descriptions and explanations that have been obtained.

▲ Basic to doing science is the generation and test of alternative explanations. Explanations are generated by use of the creative process of abduction (analogical reasoning). The initial generation of several alternatives encourages an unbiased test as one is less likely to be committed to any specific explanation. Tentative explanations are tested by use of an if-and-then-therefore reasoning pattern. A test begins by assuming that the explanation under consideration is true and by imagining some test condition(s) that allows the deduction of one or more expected results (predictions). Data (actual results) are then gathered and compared with the expected result(s). A good match provides support for the explanation, while a poor match contradicts the explanation and may lead to its rejection.

▲ Although inductively derived generalizations and explanations are both tested by use of the if-and-then-therefore reasoning pattern, generalizations and explanations are not the same thing. Generalizations (sometimes called laws) describe nature in terms of identifiable patterns (e.g., more candles make more water rise; the sun rises in the east and sets in the west; salmon spawn in their homestreams), while explanations (both hypotheses and theories) attempt to provide causes for such patterns.

▲ People do science to find out why things happen, to find causes. People want to know the causes of things to satisfy their curiosity—basic research—or so that their new knowledge can be

put to practical use—applied research.

▲ Like hypotheses, theories are explanations of nature. But while hypotheses attempt to explain a specific observation, or a group of closely related observations, theories attempt to explain broad classes of related observations, hence tend to be more general, more complex, and more abstract.

▲ Theory testing, like hypothesis testing, involves use of if-and-then-therefore reasoning. But because of the additional complexity, theories can seldom be tested in their entirety. Rather, they most often are tested component by component. Further, because of the additional abstractness, theory testing often requires the inclusion of a theoretical rationale, which links abstract and non-observable (i.e., theoretical) causal agents with observable experimental manipulations (independent variables).

▲ Theory testing may be further complicated when an advocate of a contradicted theory decides to modify, rather than reject, the theory. The modification may involve a change in a basic component, or the addition of new components. Modifications are intended to keep the theory consistent with the evidence. Nevertheless, theories that meet with repeated contradiction are generally replaced, particularly when a reasonable noncontradicted alternative exists.

▲ Although it is common practice to speak as though entities such as oxygen and carbon dioxide have been "discovered" in a manner similar to the way someone discovers a lost treasure, this practice is misleading. Instead, entities such as oxygen and carbon dioxide, like the vital force and phlogiston, can be better understood as conceptual inventions, albeit conceptual inventions that have been so thoroughly tested that their existence is no longer in question.

▲ Because any two hypotheses or theoretical claims may lead deductively to

the same expected result, observation of that result can not tell you which hypothesis or theoretical claim is correct. For this reason, supportive evidence can not prove that a hypothesis or theory is correct.

▲ Contradictory evidence can arise because of either an incorrect hypothesis/theory or a faulty test (e.g., one in which not all other variables were held constant). Further, because it is not possible to be certain that all other variables were in fact held constant, contradictory evidence can not prove that a hypothesis or theory is incorrect.

▲ Science and religion are fundamentally different "ways of knowing." Science asks that one generate alternative explanations and then consult nature as a way of testing the alternatives. Scientific knowledge, which must remain somewhat tentative, comes at the end of the process. On the other hand, religion asks that one accept a particular explanation at the outset based on faith. Nature need not be consulted and religious knowledge is considered absolute.

CONCLUSIONS AND RECOMMENDATIONS

In conclusion, it should be pointed out that the above list of statements about the nature of science represent generalizations, and as such can be learned only superficially from single-shot instruction, such as the candle-burning lab, no matter how engaging it may be. Both developmental theory and experience argue that learning about the nature of science and developing theoretical reasoning abilities are long-term propositions, which, like learning to draw in a mirror, require repeated attempts in a variety of contexts.

Indeed, the problem is compounded by the fact that students often encounter misleading statements about the nature of science, not only from television reports and newspaper articles claiming that science has proved, or disproved, such and such, but even from science textbook authors and teachers. Most likely you have seen textbook authors claim that with mounting supporting evidence hypotheses become theories, which in turn become laws, or give examples of the scientific method in which they fail to recognize the crucial difference between hypotheses and predictions (cf. Gibbs and Lawson 1992).

What college student has not heard about null hypotheses, which are not hypotheses at all. Instead they are null predictions (e.g., no significant difference should be found in the incidence of connective-tissue disease between women with and without breast implants). Little wonder that many students—and the general public—are often confused.

Another problem is that many instructors "cover" so much content that they do not leave time to discuss issues related to the nature of science. Also, the lab is often seen as an opportunity to support lecture topics rather than do real inquiries. To help solve this problem in our nonmajor courses, we no longer try to closely articulate lecture and lab so that when students need to take two or three weeks to answer a particularly difficult question in lab, they can take the time to do so.

Another threat to success is the current rush to incorporate high-tech machines such as computers and videodisc players into instructional settings. These devices may prove beneficial, but only so long as they do not replace actual hands-on, minds-on inquiries that allow students to generate and test alternative hypotheses and theories. Indeed, we would do well to keep firmly in mind the American Association for the Advancement of Science's central teaching principle which states that: "Teaching should be consistent with the nature of scientific inquiry" (AAAS 1989).

Many introductory college biology courses suffer from another problem. Having been designed largely by subject-matter experts, the courses are often structured to make sense from an already knowledgeable instructor's perspective, but not necessarily from an inquiring learner's perspective. Thus,

the courses typically take a "micro-to-macro" approach, which begins at the highly-abstract and theoretical atomic and molecular levels and only later addresses more familiar and less abstract topics at the organism, population, and community levels.

Some recent textbooks have tried to remedy this problem by taking a "macro-to-micro" approach. Thus, they start big at the biome level and work their way down to ecosystems, communities, populations, organisms, and so forth. But this approach also fails to recognize that inquiry progresses from the familiar and concrete to the unfamiliar and abstract. Students are organisms, not biomes, so student inquiries should start at the organism level and then move toward either progressively smaller or progressively larger levels of organization.

Indeed, here the history of science has much to offer in terms of helping us identify "natural" routes of inquiry, routes that past scientists have taken and routes that present students can also take—routes that should lead to scientific literacy. That is, to students who know what science is and how to do it. ❑

Note

This material is based upon research partially supported by the National Science Foundation under grant No. DUE 9453610. Any opinions, findings, and conclusions or recommendations expressed in this publication are those of the author and do not necessarily reflect the views of the National Science Foundation.

References

American Association for the Advancement of Science. 1928. On the place of science education. *School Science and Mathematics* 28:640-664.

American Association for the Advancement of Science. 1989. *Science For All Americans*. Washington, D.C.: Author.

American Association for the Advancement of Science. 1990. *The Liberal Art of Science*. Washington, D.C.: Author.

Dawson, C. J., and J. A. Rowell. 1986. All other things being equal: A study of science graduates solving control of variables problems. *Research in Science and Technological Education* 4:49-60.

Educational Policies Commission. 1961. *The Central Purpose of American Education*. Washington, D.C.: National Education Association.

Educational Policies Commission. 1966. *Education and the Spirit of Science*. Washington, D.C.: National Education Association.

Elementary Science Study. 1974. *Attribute Games and Problems: Teachers' Guide*. New York: McGraw Hill.

Feynman, R. P. 1966. What is science? Paper presented at the Fourteenth Annual Convention, National Science Teachers Association, New York City, April 1-5.

Gibbs, A., and A. E. Lawson. 1992. The nature of scientific thinking as reflected by the work of biologists and biology textbooks. *The American Biology Teacher* 54(3): 137-152.

Inhelder, B., and J. Piaget. 1958. *The Growth of Logical Thinking from Childhood to Adolescence*. New York: Basic Books.

Karplus, R., A. E. Lawson, W. Wollman, M. Appel, R. Bernoff, A. Howe, J. J. Rusch, and F. Sullivan. 1977. *Science Teaching and the Development of Reasoning*. Berkeley, CA: Regents of the University of California.

Lawson, A. E. 1992. The development of reasoning among college biology students—A review of research. *Journal of College Science Teaching* 21(6): 338-344.

Lawson, A. E. 1993. Deductive reasoning, brain maturation, and science concept acquisition: Are they linked? *Journal of Research in Science Teaching* 30(9): 1029-1952.

Lawson, A. E. 1994. Research on the acquisition of science knowledge:Epistemological foundations of cognition. In *Handbook of Research on Science Teaching and Learning*, ed. D. L. Gabel. New York: Macmillan.

Lawson, A. E., N. Drake, J. Johnson, Y. J. Kwon, and C. Scarpone. 1997. The development of scientific thinking skills: Is there a fifth stage? Paper presented at the Annual Convention, National Association for Research in Science Teaching, Oak Brook, IL, March 21-24.

Lederman, N. G. 1992. Students' and teachers' conceptions of the nature of science: A review of the research. *Journal of Research in Science Teaching* 29:331-359.

Mackay, L. D. 1971. Development of understanding about the nature of science.*Journal of Research in Science Teaching* 8:57-66.

National Assessment of Educational Progress. 1988. *Science Objectives: 1985-86 Assessment* (Objectives booklet No. 17-S-10). Princeton, NJ: Author.

National Research Council. 1995. *National Science Education Standards*. Washington, D.C.: National Academy Press.

National Science Foundation. 1996. *Shaping the Future*. Washington, D.C.: Author.

National Society for the Study of Education. 1960. *Rethinking Science Education* (59th yearbook, Part I). Chicago: University of Chicago Press.

Peckham, G. D. 1993. A new use for the candle and tumbler myth. *Journal of Chemical Education* 70(12): 1008-1009.

Piaget, J. 1971. Problems of equilibration. In *Piaget and Inhelder on Equilibration*, eds. C. F. Nodine, J. M. Gallagher, and R. D. Humphreys. Philadelphia, PA: The Jean Piaget Society.

Piaget, J., and B. Inhelder. 1969. *The Psychology of the Child*. New York: Basic Books.

Ryan, A. G., and G. S. Aikenhead. 1992. Students preconceptions about the epistemology of science. *Science Education* 76:559-580.

Walker, R. A. 1979. Formal operational reasoning patterns and scholastic achievement in genetics. *Journal of College Science Teaching* 8:156-168.

A Science-in-the-Making Course for Nonscience Majors

Reinforcing the Scientific Method Using an Inquiry Approach

Deborah A. Tolman

Using the inquiry method, nonscience majors in Portland State University's Natural Science Inquiry classes complete student-directed projects, individually and in groups, that tackle scientific, ethical, political, and social issues. By observing, problem solving, and making sense of data, students play a more active role in their science education.

Imagine this: a college classroom of nonscience majors has just been given a set of water quality data from a large watershed project. The data consist of 32 variables, ranging from dissolved oxygen and ammonium/nitrate content to soluble phosphorus and orthophosphorus. The data are raw; they were taken by two different consulting groups and often have gaps in sample times.

The students are arranged in small groups for this project. Although they have prepared for this moment by performing a series of activities designed to develop their skills, for now their only instructions are to make sense of the data.

For the first five minutes their reaction is silence. It is silence of the worst kind for an instructor who wants to either push them in the right direction or fill the quiet by telling them how to begin to produce an arguable case for their findings.

Soon the energy level starts to rise. Mumblings of frustrations can be heard from the once-hushed group. Questions ensue about what will be expected from the instructor, their peers, and themselves. The instructor responds with encouragement: they are to explore every path in considering a problem that may not have answers except those the students discover for themselves. In this way, they will be the scientists.

At hearing this, some students still express frustration, but the rest of the group moves quickly to decide where to begin, what steps to take—and avoid—and how to manage such an overwhelming project. This stage is the beginning of valuable self-development that lies beneath the inquiry process of "doing science."

Too often in college-level science classes students must rely on the lecture format to learn scientific concepts and facts about the natural world. They also have to be able to recall facts without using their own input or conducting their own critical inspection of the process. However, this does not approximate the process used by a scientist. Scientific discovery operates in a different manner. Facts are merely resting points until a new discovery is made, and science holds an interpretation of nature that is subject to alteration.

With today's controversies on the use of science in resolving societal issues, it is the argument itself that we should be teaching in the classroom (Thomas 1980). Contained in that argument are the observations, the inquiry, the fact finding, and the communication of the scientific method.

In this article, I outline projects of a broader context in a college-level science course for nonscience majors. These projects encourage students to immerse themselves in the project, giving them a more active role in their sci-

Deborah A. Tolman is a research assistant, Center for Science Education, Portland State University, PO Box 751, Portland, OR 97207; e-mail: psu03187@odin.cc.pdx.edu.

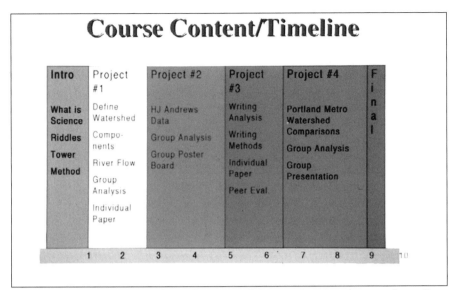

Course Content/Timeline

Intro	Project #1	Project #2	Project #3	Project #4	Final
What is Science	Define Watershed	HJ Andrews Data	Writing Analysis	Portland Metro Watershed Comparisons	F i n a l
Riddles	Components	Group Analysis	Writing Methods	Group Analysis	
Tower	River Flow	Group Poster Board	Individual Paper	Group Presentation	
Method	Group Analysis		Peer Eval.		
	Individual Paper				

| 1 | 2 | 3 | 4 | 5 | 6 | 7 | 8 | 9 | 10 |

A sample course content outline of a Natural Science Inquiry class taught at Portland State University in Oregon.

ence education.

Within this framework, the Science for the Liberal Arts Curriculum (SLA) at Portland State University offers Natural Science Inquiry (NSI) classes to sophomore-level students of all disciplines. Employing the inquiry method, the NSI instructors involve students in practicing science and discovering its uncertainties. Three student-directed projects enable the students to think critically and create their own paths to reaching conclusions or "knowledge claims."

In the NSI projects, students observe, make sense of data, and learn how the natural world is generally interpreted. In additional mini-projects, students tackle ethical, political, and social issues both individually and as members of a group.

While carrying out these projects, the students uncover the basic principles of the scientific method in a style that is intellectually stimulating and enjoyable.

For example, instead of presenting the scientific method as an isolated concept, students are given data, asked to graph it in any manner they see fit, and, by following their hunches, make stabs at where the data may lead. They are instructed to make educated guesses and/or describe what they ob-

serve and support it with their findings. This aspect of the scientific method is reinforced by class discussions, formal and informal writing assignments, computer usage, Internet browsing, and team work.

INSTITUTIONAL CONTEXT

The SLA curriculum, part of a university-wide reform of general education requirements (White 1994), is the key science component of general studies at Portland State University. The three clusters of SLA courses—Natural Science Inquiry, Integrated Science Concepts, and Context of Science in Society—are designed to focus on general characteristics of science-in-the-making, that is, the process of active scientific inquiry.

Central to all the courses are "natural science communities of inquiry" that involve investigative laboratories and field studies and/or research projects, and that focus on scientific processes of problem-posing, problem-solving, and persuasion. In general, the classes emphasize the ability to work with facts rather than the facts themselves.

Students are encouraged to debate interpretations of data as well as their personal opinions on pressing scientific, political, economic, social, and

ethical issues. Key instructional features of SLA courses include "doing science as science is done," allowing the nature of the inquiry to set the direction of the course and most of the course content, working in collaborative research teams, ensuring that inquiry is open-ended, and using a variety of formal and informal writing techniques.

NATURAL SCIENCE INQUIRY

The quarter begins with a short introduction to the scientific method using *A Handbook of Biological Investigation, Fifth Edition* (Ambrose III et al. 1995). The students also read Connolly's (1989) *Writing and the Ecology of Learning* to acquaint themselves with the everyday nature of critical analysis, whether in the classroom or in their personal lives.

The inquiry process is continually reinforced by reflective writing in journals that can be discussed in later class periods. The instructor distributes several articles, which change every quarter, from a wide variety of journals to serve as examples of formal writing and to distinguish popular journal articles from peer-reviewed scientific ones. But these articles are only guides. The true learning experience comes from the writing process.

Below are samples of some of the many projects offered in an NSI course. These courses are still in the experimental stages. The description of the course is broken down into three parts to give the reader an idea of the timetable and emphasis in the inquiry process. Please note that some assignments may overlap.

Part 1: Making Knowledge Claims. For the first three weeks of a 10-week course, we try to remove any preconceived fears of science using projects that place every student on the same level of expertise. The projects center around doing science and strategies for working in groups.

For example, students in groups are asked to record as many observations as possible relying only on the taste, smell, sight, or sound of an unknown object or an ailing plant. These exercises capture the importance of imagination and creativity in science. The students collaborate freely, outside their discipline, their culture, and their level of experience to name the object or the ailment. The instructor then asks the group to draw up questions to pose to an expert that would help determine the accuracy of their guesses.

Reduced to making guesses based on sensory perceptions, the students encounter their biases of what they do or do not believe. This is an opportunity for the instructor to dispel some of the subjective views that may follow the students' inductive reasoning.

Students should be aware that biases often result from making general assumptions about a case after only having observed a few such cases. Knowledge claims that require more than a single observation are often easy to construct but can also easily be challenged by peers in the context of larger class discussions. These discussions, which occur early in the quarter, can be facilitated by asking the following questions: Are knowledge claims in science different than in other fields? How much authority is required to make a claim?

Another project is a weather data set. Students are given rain, solar, barometric, wind speed, wind direction, and humidity measurements of a particular day and asked to characterize the day or put it into "real description," that is, nontechnical, experiential, or sensory language. This task can be very challenging because it requires students to sort out the superfluous information and organize the relevant data.

As they dig and investigate, they often find that graphing one variable is not as accurate a picture of the day as graphing combinations of variables. To add to their confusion, we like to offer two "good" data sets along with two sets of "bad" data (those with equipment error) of the same day.

The presence of "bad" data serves a twofold purpose: it enables students to make additional inferences about precision and accuracy of the instruments that collected the data, and it forces the students to use more data sets to confirm any inferences about the inaccuracy of instruments. They must decide which variables are pertinent and which deal with uncertainty.

The students discover for themselves that although weather variables may conform to basic science concepts, they often interact simultaneously in very unpredictable and chaotic ways.

We believe that Portland State's Natural Science Inquiry courses, through the spirit of investigation, are one way of connecting students with the outside world while inside the classroom.

The project also requires sorting through lots of information from a variety of sources (both inside and outside the classroom) and choosing relevant information on weather, discussing it with group members, and making inferences with supporting arguments. Each of these early projects provides a good foundation for the discovery process.

In the weather project, students collaborate to arrive at a consensus on the particular unknown day. At the close of the process, students are asked their biases, objectivity, authority, strong and weak inferences, and any a priori information that affected the investigation. By the end of the project, they have made guesses at the data, inferred a particular season, described the day in question, and anticipated any changes such as fronts moving through

the area.

The instructor provides simple statistics to describe the strangeness of the day, for example, correlation, patterns, trends, and the computer skills necessary to extract information, as well as answers to basic questions on weather concepts that are not located on the Internet.

As final assignments, the students present a poster session on inferences on the weather data, submit a formal scientific paper on this topic, and complete reflective thinking exercises in the journals.

Students rely heavily on *A Handbook of Biological Investigation* during the beginning of the quarter, and the instructor provides journal prompts to help with the reflection process. Examples of good journal starters at this point in the course are:
▲ What did you do and how did you go about it?
▲ Did you "do science"? Why or why not?
▲ Are there examples of "good" science or "bad" science?
▲ If so, write convincing arguments that support either your "good" or "bad" examples.
▲ What advances did you make in arriving at an inference?
▲ What information did you gain by graphing two weather variables together?
▲ What level of uncertainty are you willing to accept?
▲ Under what circumstances is this level acceptable/not acceptable? In preparation for the next project, we ask the students to consider what method of collaboration works or does not work for them and why.

Part 2: Critically Analyzing Information. During the next two to three weeks of the course, the instructor focuses on the idea that claims can be refuted from two sides. To understand this notion, students must prepare a three-page essay on a controversial science topic. They do not work in groups for this project. The papers must present both pro- and counterarguments for the topic. Ultimately, they must persuade the reader in one direction or the other.

As a class, we examine the different methods of persuasion found in popular articles, newspapers, and scientific articles. These articles help students determine how much information they will need to gather for their argument and counterargument.

At the same time, questions arise concerning hypothesis statements—how should they look and how are they different from inferences. These

Students in a Portland State University Natural Science Inquiry class determining connections between watersheds, topography, and urban areas.

concerns are explored during journal readings followed by lengthy discussions about the use of authority and human emotion in persuasive essays. At this point, acting out a controversial topic in class can help students see the different angles used in building a case.

Part 3: Frame a Problem, Observe, Inquire, Infer, and Substantiate an Inference. For the remaining weeks, students prepare for the largest project of the quarter by working in groups to interpret the data. This project varies according to NSI instructor, but it is always linked to social, political, eco-

nomic, and philosophical contexts. The project has concrete goals but is purposely nonspecific in its method and final product. In this way, it is all student directed and emphasizes the best of an investigation that involves "...starting with hunches, making guesses (most of which prove to be wild), making many mistakes, going off on blind roads before hitting on one that seems to be going in the right direction" (Hildebrand 1957, 7).

In one class, the students write and publish an environmental awareness booklet that is disseminated to the citizens of Portland, Oregon. The *Portland Today* project guides public understanding of current problems during a time when the city is crafting an environmental quality index. The students consider such issues as population, land use, air quality, energy consumption, water quality, neighborhood involvement, fish and wildlife, transportation, recycling, and hazardous wastes. The project's purpose is to:

> improve the community's awareness of the urban environment in the Portland metropolitan area. Our goal is not only to familiarize, but hopefully to motivate the citizens of Portland to become involved in maintaining, protecting, or improving dif-

ferent aspects of Portland's environment (Caleen and Wruck 1996).

The project encompasses all the elements of a scientific investigation, giving students a true feel for collecting, sorting, and distinguishing between "good" and "bad" data, determining how much data is enough, what indicators are important, and who the audience is, and examining the dilemma that most cities face, that is, how to cope with increasing demands on natural resources.

The students work in various capacities with city officials representing 16 different agencies in the Portland area. The final project, due at the end of the quarter, is a presentation from each group complete with their portion of the environmental awareness booklet. A few students, in another class for additional course credit, do the typesetting and prepare the booklet for the printer. The document is released on Earth Day, April 22, to promote the environmental health and sustainability of Portland.

In another NSI final project, students explore original United States Forest Service data on either gravel size in streams, stream temperature, or woody debris in streams. The instructor intentionally lets the students "go" in this self-directed project, taking on a facilitative role and giving students center stage. In such an independent project, students must be creative in finding relationships with the data, which can be frustrating if no relationships are present.

At this point, the instructor reminds them of alternative hypotheses that may be important in their findings: if data doesn't infer anything, does it disprove something? With this guidance, students have responded by channeling their frustrations to produce meaningful scientific papers complete with abstract, materials and methods section, results, and concluding remarks.

ASSESSMENT

There are no exams in the NSI courses. Student achievement is

Table 1. NSI Assessment Foci

SLA Cluster Course	Predominant Theme	Techniques	Assessment			
			Application of Scientific Content & Concept	Formulation of Question	Design of Investigation	Analysis & Interpretation
NSI	Using Watersheds to Teach the Scientific Method & Critical Thinking to Non Science Majors	1) 4 freewrites in all 4 class assessment areas 2) freewrites in field-based assessment as well 3) concept maps	X	X	X	
NSI	Issues in Forest Ecosystems	1) minute freewrites re: class hurdles, most memorable experiences, and key teaching approaches 2) personal interviews by anonymous interviewer 3) prior knowledge probes 4) debates	X			X
NSI	Climatology	1) periodic classroom ass. techniques combined with classroom feedback tech.	X	X	X	X
NSI	Issues around Water Quality	1) preclass and postclass reading of the same scientific article w/ questions	X	X		

assessed based on written research papers (one individual essay and two group papers), class participation, and journal entries. The instructor monitors student Internet competency and computer graphics skills on a weekly basis. In addition to these assessments, a poster session is required and graded in Part I of the course. The formal scientific paper is required in Part III, along with a presentation on the final day of the quarter. These presentations enable students to share their experience with their peers and confirm their findings publicly. As instructors, we feel that this is an important part of the self-development process.

The instructor also evaluates aspects of the course for their effectiveness. For example, one goal is to understand scientific information from direct sources. To test this skill, the instructor gives each student a journal article to read independently twice a term. The articles are chosen for their relevance to the course content and written at a level appropriate for first-year college students.

After reading through the article, students are asked to freewrite for 10 minutes addressing several questions such as: What do you understand from reading the article? What is the author's hypothesis? How did you read the article to make sense of it? What additional information might you need to better understand the article?

Students are asked to read aloud from their freewrites. They then form small groups and read portions of the article again, perhaps aloud, and address the same questions within their groups. These questions are discussed with the class as a whole. At the end of the discussion, students do another five to 10 minute freewrite on what they now understand about the article and the ways in which they are making sense of it. Through this process, we can assess changes in students' ability to interpret scientific information (Ramette 1995).

Instructors have experimented with other techniques to assess the course's effectiveness (see **Table 1**). One technique that appears useful is a 10-question self-assessment of learning gains provided at the beginning and again at the end of the quarter. This method addresses students' comprehension of a scientific article through questions designed to check logical scientific methods.

For example, asking students to summarize their understanding of an article tests their ability to sort out the most important claims. Asking what terms or symbols either helped or hindered a complete understanding of the claims can identify the key relationships that may be missing from the article. Writing about the claim that they found to be most interesting or significant and the process through which the authors arrived at the claim helps instructors assess weaknesses and strengths in the students' scientific logic and underlying assumptions.

Researchers have found that instructional methodologies that allow individuals to "do science" and use their sensory perception of the process leads to higher science achievement (Koballa 1986). All techniques used in the 1993-94, 1994-95, and 1995-96 school years confirm that students taking the NSI courses—in contrast to students in standard lecture-format science courses—show a marked improvement in their appreciation of science and their ability to see the relevance of science to their lives.

The students also exhibited a marked decrease in their fear of math and science courses. By doing the inquiry process in class, the students have

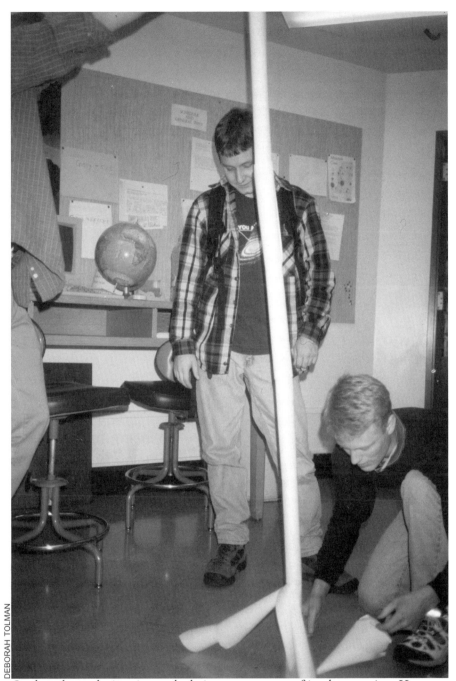

DEBORAH TOLMAN

Students learn the inquiry method via an assortment of in-class exercises. Here, students are exploring the best way to construct a free-standing paper tower.

lems in science. The course curriculum is imperative for classes in which students reflect, collaborate, communicate, and direct their own learning about science.

Future NSI classes will introduce students to data collecting, the next logical step. If students can observe the field that produced the data, perhaps they can provide the link to obtaining quantitative data and making quantitative claims based on observation.

We know that we have a long way to go before students are sufficiently critical thinkers to understand the mysteries and profound paradoxes of science. But we believe that the NSI courses, through the spirit of investigation, are one way of connecting them with the outside world while inside the classroom. ❑

References

Ambrose III, Harrison W., and Katharine Peckham Ambrose. 1995. *A Handbook of Biological Investigation, Fifth Edition.* Winston-Salem, NC: Hunter Textbooks Inc.

Caleen, Cheryl, and Linda Wruck, eds. 1996. *Portland Today.* Portland, OR: Portland State University, Center for Science Education.

Connolly, Paul. 1989. Writing and the ecology of learning. In *Writing to Learn Mathematics and Science*, eds. Paul Connolly and Teresa Vilardi. New York: Teachers College Press.

Koballa, T. R., Jr. 1986. Teaching hands-on science activities: Variables that moderate attitude-behavior consistency. *Journal of Research in Science Teaching* 23(6): 493-502.

Ramette, Cheryl. 1995. Curriculum Analyst, Office of University Studies, Portland State University, Portland, OR. Personal Communication.

Ramette, Cheryl. 1998. Curriculum Analyst, Office of University Studies, Portland State University, Portland, OR. Personal Communication.

Thomas, Lewis. 1980. *Late Night Thoughts on Listening to Mahler's Ninth Symphony.* New York: The Viking Press.

White, Charles R. 1994. A model for comprehensive reform in general education: Portland State University. *Journal of General Education* 43(3): 168-229.

developed a much keener appreciation of science. This response is evidenced by increased enrollment in these classes and students' positive feedback in interviews, journal writings, and course evaluations (Ramette 1998).

These NSI classes may hold promise not only for nonmajors but also for majors who lack proper grounding in the scientific method. The teaching techniques used in these classes are appropriate for courses that require students to think critically and creatively in making decisions and solving prob-

Investigative Learning in Undergraduate Freshman Biology Laboratories

A Pilot Project at Virginia Tech—New Roles for Students and Teachers in an Experimental Design Laboratory

George E. Glasson and Woodrow L. McKenzie

What turned these kids on is an investigative approach, where they can do the thinking,...and I like that approach too.

—Art Buikema, Biology Professor

A professor, frustrated with traditional "cookbook" laboratory exercises—assignments that lead students through prescribed laboratory procedures to confirm existing knowledge as presented in the teacher's lectures—spoke these words.

Professor Arthur Buikema and his graduate teaching assistant (TA), Rhonda Wilhite, collaborated to develop new laboratory activities that emphasize investigation and experimental design. Their efforts were part of V-QUEST, a project supported by the National Science Foundation's systemic reform initiative (cooperative

George E. Glasson is an associate professor of science education, department of teaching and learning, Virginia Tech, Blacksburg, VA 24061-0313. Woodrow L. McKenzie is an instructor, department of chemistry and physics, Radford University, Radford, VA 24142.

agreement #OSR 9250058). In this project, faculty studied their existing curriculum and made changes resulting from reflection on teaching methodologies, collaboration with other teachers, and testing of new strategies in the classroom.

Faculty focused on changing the laboratory component of a freshman biology course from a didactic, teacher-directed approach to one in which students became investigative learners by formulating hypotheses and testing their ideas. As part of the assessment of the project, the authors studied these learning transformations during one laboratory investigation by videotaping classroom interactions, interviewing students and faculty, and analyzing examples of student work. In the case study that follows, data were synthesized to determine: the perspectives of the professor, TA, and students concerning the implementation of investigative laboratories, and the classroom interactions and student learning that took place.

Although the advantages of investigative laboratories have already been documented (Leonard 1989; Deutch 1994, Stukus and Lennox 1995), this report is unique because it focuses on

changing faculty perspectives and student learning during investigative laboratory instruction.

A PROFESSOR'S PERSPECTIVE ON INVESTIGATIVE LEARNING

As part of the V-QUEST project activities, participating faculty and TAs attended summer staff development sessions on various topics relating to investigative learning, alternative assessment, and learning enhancement of minorities in science classes. During the fall, after having attended these sessions, a biology professor was interviewed as he was attempting to change his approach to teaching:

> When I first taught honors biology, I lectured....One day I walked in and I said 'I don't like coming to class. You're very bright people...but something is missing here'...and they helped me design the class....I had to learn that I had to trust myself that I didn't have to be perfect, that I could make mistakes, that I could hypothesize too.

For many professors, the shift from teacher-centered to learner-centered instruction is difficult because teachers have to change with the students. As students become the creators of their own education, the teacher no longer predetermines the direction of inquiry that the students may take on a given day. The teacher must not only relinquish that sense of authority, but must also behave as a scientist in the presence of the students. Scientific thought and its fallibility are thus modeled. For many, this new, additional role of teacher as learner may seem an awkward and unwelcome loss of control.

However, the professor's success in transforming his freshman honors biology course led him to speculate that all freshman biology students could succeed with a similar approach. He subsequently received permission to implement investigative laboratory exercises (developed as part of the V-QUEST activities) in the freshman general biology (nonmajor) and principles of biology (major) courses. These courses enrolled approximately 2,100 students. Traditionally, the courses have included a heavy dose of content material in lecture and two-hour "cookbook" laboratory exercises containing proceduralized, corroborative exercises that usually require the entire period to complete with little time for mistakes or repetition.

A TA was chosen to pilot the new, investigative approach during the summer "Principles of Biology" course. She met with the professor every two weeks to reevaluate and reassess several investigative laboratory activities. These preliminary trials were encouraging and plans were made to implement the changes in the fall semester.

Though the professor had confidence in the TA who piloted the labs, he was initially concerned about how the other TAs, who would be teaching the fall biology courses, would accept the change. Early in the fall, the professor met with the TAs and discussed his concerns:

> I went in there and talked about the problems, the frustrations, how you answer a question with a question, without getting them so upset with you, they're going to turn you off....When I got done, I walked out of that TA meeting and I said..."I don't think these TAs are with us." I don't know. I did not walk out of there feeling comfortable.

Despite initial reservations among the TAs, the professor was willing to risk moving towards more learner-centered instruction. A description of an investigative laboratory activity used in the biology classes follows.

Respiration Laboratory: In this laboratory activity, students investigated the respiration of yeast. The instructor challenged them to hypothesize and develop their own experiments while working in collaborative groups. The handout for the respiration lab consisted of a page of background information on the topics of "Energetics: Anaerobic Metabolism" and "Fermentation." However, the laboratory procedure differed significantly from more conventional ones, as students were asked to "speculate why the alcohol content of naturally aged wines is between 12 and 14 percent alcohol (even though there may be sugar remaining in the brewing mixture)."

Students were also asked to "design an experiment to look at the effects of alcohol concentration on the fermentation ability of yeast." Students had to formulate and test a hypothesis, include control groups, record and graph data, and interpret results. Students employed materials and equipment made available to them on tables (see **Appendix A**).

Videotaped Classroom Interactions: The TA spent about 20 minutes reviewing the concepts of respiration and fermentation, including glycolysis, before letting the students begin. Students read their texts prior to class and were exposed to the material in the lecture section of the class. The TA ended the review and started the lab with the following question and comments:

> Can you speculate why the alcohol content of naturally aged wines is between 12 and 14 percent alcohol, even though there may be sugar remaining in the growth mixture? Okay, what you want to do is to come up with some way to find out why it is happening—you want to formulate a hypothesis as a group based on this speculation.

At this point, the room was quiet, but soon each table had students actively discussing and guessing. Students had salt, sugar, yeast, water, and etha-

nol as materials to work with and a controlled-temperature water bath. They considered all these as variables (including temperature) to be controlled as they formulated hypotheses and designed experiments to test their ideas.

As the activity proceeded, the attention focused on each student group instead of on the teacher at the front of the room. The TA roamed throughout the room listening and giving advice, sometimes guiding the group's thinking, but always letting them make their own decisions about what hypotheses should be tested or what should be altered. For example, two students were engaged in conversation while receiving guidance from their teacher:

▲ *First Student*: It's something like there's so much alcohol in there, it's like a feedback inhibition....

▲ *Second Student*: And too much alcohol can poison all that. Maybe that's the point where yeast die.

▲ *First Student*: Like when you make bread?

▲ *TA*: Okay. Right. What are you given here to look at? (They point to water bath.)

▲ *Second Student*: To test at different temperatures....

▲ *TA*: Okay, now how would this affect the level of alcohol production?

▲ *First Student*: It speeds up the reaction....

The TA continued to prompt students to think about experimental design:

▲ *TA*: Let's talk about your methodology....How are you going to do this? What percentage of alcohol, what amount of alcohol are you going to have in each test tube; and you're going to want to figure out how you're going to do this.

As might be expected, each group of students came up with a different experiment. They were encouraged to use controls and to work with variables they could measure, but final decisions were left to them.

As the discussions continued, the TA grappled with the problem of how much guidance to offer the students. For example, one group of students considered controlling the concentration of water in test tube cultures of the yeast as a variable, since water was one of the materials supplied for the lab. Another group wondered what they could learn by varying the salt concentration of the cultures. Would this be time well spent in a learning endeavor even though the stated purpose of the lab was to look at alcohol concentration? In each case, the TA did her best to answer the students' questions without giving them directions for experimental design. This process took most of the time remaining in the two-hour period, and most

treatments to begin with. Students were evaluated on whether they were able to come up with a testable hypothesis and follow through with an experiment in which they were able to control variables, graph and interpret results, analyze what they would do differently, and present their findings in a concise and coherent report.

Student Laboratory Reports: According to the TA, the results documented in student laboratory reports as tables and graphs "were all over the place." The results of two student groups are given below as examples of student-learning experimental design.

Group I came up with the following testable hypothesis and provided

tion of ethanol between 16.7 percent and 25 percent stops fermentation. Even more important, in terms of demonstrating their learning of science, were their suggestions on how to improve the experiment if they had the chance to repeat it. The students stated that they would fine tune their procedure so they could more precisely "determine the actual concentration of ethanol at which fermentation stops."

Group II tested a hypothesis that focused on the amount of yeast as a variable: During fermentation, the amount of yeast used is directly related to the amount of carbon dioxide produced. The more yeast used, the more CO_2 produced.

During their first trial, they did not observe carbon dioxide being produced and correctly concluded that their yeast was inactive. However, in the second trial, they found that as the amount of yeast increased, the CO_2 produced increased. Thus, they concluded that the amount of yeast was the limiting variable in determining the percentage of alcohol in wine. The students also stated, "the presence of alcohol should not affect the production of CO_2 because alcohol is another product caused by the fermentation of yeast." Although both groups were successful in developing testable hypotheses, the misconceptions of group II were clarified by the TA during class discussions.

Reflections on Respiration Lab: Instructors interviewed the students after the respiration lab to gain insight into investigative teaching approaches. The following are the comments of two students:

▲ *First Student:* That one was easy to remember because you had to actually make up the experiment yourself, you didn't just do an experiment that was given to you in a lab book.

▲ *Second Student:* Respiration? Okay, actually I enjoyed that a lot more than the previous labs that we've done because we actually had to come up with the experiment and hypothesis. It wasn't just like a textbook, you know, read this and follow this and record your results. We actually got

Professor Buikema and Rhonda Wilhite (in background) advise students performing an experiment on the respiration of yeast during a laboratory class at Virginia Tech.

of the groups did not actually carry out the experiment until the following week.

Assessment: Although each group was testing different factors and reaching different conclusions, they were able to present and share their designs and findings. During this time, the TA discussed the design and limitations of each experiment in relation to the original speculation. Many of the students reported that a retrial of their experiments would provide better data or that their experiments needed more

data to demonstrate that alcohol produced limited fermentation: When the largest amount of ethanol is added to yeast and sugar, fermentation will be decreased the most (CO_2 amount will be the least) and the yeast may be killed.

This group proceeded to vary the amount of alcohol added to a yeast solution and collected the CO_2 gas in an inverted test tube. Their results showed decreasing levels of CO_2 produced as alcohol concentration increased. The students concluded that a concentrato...test for fermentation. You come up with a hypothesis, you come up with an experiment, and you do it. You come up with the results. It was more personal and you learned more because you were the one who was coming up with everything.

These remarks reveal that students learn more about designing experiments when they take an active part in learning. More importantly, as one student put it, this type of learning is more personal because the students make their own decisions and this independent thinking stimulates learning.

The professor implemented this respiration activity in over 80 biology laboratory sections. He met regularly with the TAs to discuss the investigative approach. However, many TAs were initially reluctant to change to an investigative approach. After the respiration lab was completed, the professor shared his thoughts:

> There were some TAs that said they started in frustration but didn't end in frustration. But when one of the TAs said 'Can we do more of these?' I knew we were hooked. They were hooked!
>
> All of them took two hours to come up with the design but each group of undergraduates came up with a testable hypothesis—that was exciting!

It was very encouraging that the TAs wished to do more labs like this one. The TA piloting the labs reiterated her enthusiasm for investigative learning:

> I think one of the advantages of this lab is that while you're helping the students or while you're trying to lead them to come up with a hypothesis, you realize that you can try to find their weak spots. Do they understand the entire hypothesis? ... It's been promising, because before this lab I would have been hesitant to trust my students to come up with an entire lab. They actually did it!

The TAs learned how to "answer questions with questions" and encourage students to think on their own. They supplied students with the necessary tools to solve the problem, while not solving the problem for them.

DISCUSSION

In an effort to develop investigative and learner-centered laboratory activities, the biology professor was willing to "experiment" with his pedagogy and involve his TAs and students with risk taking. This approach to reforming laboratory instruction requires faculty and students to deal with uncertainty and ambiguity. For example, both the TAs and students were unsure of the outcome of the experiments that were designed. This open-ended problem-solving approach requires extra time to let students think, test their ideas, have false starts, make mistakes, and redo experiments. The TAs were also engaged in speculative problem-solving as they guided students in designing experiments. Modeling speculative, hypothetical thought is essential to help students proceed with open-ended investigation.

When students hypothesized, tested their ideas, examined sources of information, designed experiments, and proposed explanations, they became engaged in scientific inquiry and ways of knowing about the natural world (AAAS 1990; NRC 1994).

During laboratory instruction, learning experimental design was more valuable than having students verify information presented in lectures. In designing their experiments, many students referred to and discussed information provided about anaerobic metabolism and fermentation. This process more closely mimics scientific investigation by encouraging students to be resourceful and by helping them make connections with useful information. In contrast, students completing confirmatory "cookbook" laboratory activities become more adept in following directions and reproducing conclusions that are accepted by the teacher.

During the investigative laboratory activities, students spent a lot of time in collaborative groups, deliberating and discussing possibilities. As they shared their experiments with each other and their TAs, students learned about respiration of yeast within the context of their own speculative ideas. Taking personal ownership of ideas is an important process step in helping students construct ideas and value their own thinking (Martin and Brouwer 1991). In the respiration laboratory, each collaborative group developed their identity by establishing ownership of their experiment.

Considering that "second tier" minority and women students are often "weeded" out of entry-level science courses (Tobias 1990; Nespor 1994), it is essential that educators explore alternative instructional strategies in which students collaborate to develop their own ideas in the process of designing experiments.

Future assessment of this project will compare learning in investigative laboratory classes with traditional laboratory classes. While investigative laboratories focus on engaging students in designing experiments, traditional laboratory procedures focus more on verifying specific scientific content. Faculty face the dilemma of deciding which learning outcomes they seek. Should they produce students who have gained prescribed knowledge or those who have learned how to be scientists? A compromise might be a combination of these techniques within laboratory instruction, realizing that students learn scientific content in the process of designing experiments.❑

References

American Association for the Advancement of Science. 1990. *Science for all Americans*. New York: Oxford Univ. Press.

Deutch, C.E. 1994. Restructuring a general microbiology laboratory into an investigative experience. *The American Biology Teacher* 56:294-296.

Leonard, W.H. 1989. Ten years of research on investigative laboratory instruction activities. *Journal of College Science Teaching* 18:304-306.

Martin, B.E., and W. Brouwer. 1991. The sharing of personal science and the narrative element in science education. *Science Education* 75(6): 707-722.

National Research Council. November, 1994. *National Science Education Standards*. Washington, DC: The National Academy of Sciences.

Nespor, J. 1994. *Knowledge in Motion: Space, Time and Curriculum in Undergraduate Physics and Management*. London: The Falmer Press.

Stukus, P., and J.E. Lennox. 1995. Use of an investigative semester-length laboratory project in an introductory microbiology course. *Journal of College Science Teaching* 25: 135-139.

Tobias, S. 1990. *They're Not Dumb, They're Different: Stalking the Second Tier*. Tucson, Ariz: Research Corporation.

Appendix A. **Description of the Respiration Lab.**

Materials:
- ▲ test tubes & racks
- ▲ assorted beakers
- ▲ graduated cylinders
- ▲ pipets
- ▲ small tubes for measuring gas displacement
- ▲ controlled temperature water bath
- ▲ sugar
- ▲ salt
- ▲ distilled water
- ▲ 50% ethanol
- ▲ labeling materials
- ▲ activated yeast cultures

Before beginning this lab exercise, review your text book and lecture notes for more information on metabolism (respiration) and the organelles of the cells where metabolism occurs. Discuss the process among your group members.

Purpose of the Laboratory:

To design an experiment to look at the effects of alcohol concentration on the fermentation ability of yeast.

Speculation:

Consider the difference between naturally aged and fortified wines. Can you speculate why the alcohol content of naturally aged wines is between 12 and 14 alcohol (even though there may be sugar remaining in the brewing mixture)?

Experimental Design:

- ▲ Reword your speculation as a scientific hypothesis that can be tested.
- ▲ Your group must design an experiment to test your hypothesis. All of the equipment you will need is available at your table. Your design must include appropriate controls. Once you have designed your experiment, share it with the instructor before you begin the experiment.
- ▲ Describe your experimental design (materials and methods).
- ▲ Record your raw data in Table 1. Be sure to include column headings so that you remember what your data represent.
- ▲ Present your raw data as a graph(s). Give each graph a title and number (*i.e.,* Figure 1, 2, 3 etc.). Be sure all axes are labeled correctly.
- ▲ Describe your results (graphs). Do not explain results at this point.
- ▲ How do you interpret (explain) the results that you obtained?
- ▲ What are your conclusions?
- ▲ Were you able to defend your hypothesis?
- ▲ If you were to do the experiment again, what would your group do differently and why?

Use of an Investigative Semester-Length Laboratory Project in an Introductory Microbiology Course

Acquainting Students with the Research Process and the Scientific Frame of Mind

Philip Stukus and John E. Lennox

American students are poorly prepared to enter the science, mathematics, and technology workforce. This conclusion has been borne out by many studies of the current state of United States science education. Although these studies were commissioned separately and had varying sponsorship, with differing client populations, the similarity in their recommendations is noteworthy.

Three of these reports, *Project 2061: Fulfilling the Promise, Biology Education in the Nation's Schools,* and *The Liberal Art of Science: Agenda for Action,* present a wide array of suggestions for revamping precollege and college science curricula. In addition, each noted an overemphasis on science content and a lack of attention to the process and unifying concepts. These studies

Philip Stukus is a professor of biology at Denison University, Granville, OH 43023. John E. Lennox is an associate professor of microbiology at The Pennsylvania State University–Altoona Campus, Altoona, PA 16603.

make the following three major recommendations for faculty and curricula:

▲ Increase laboratory experience, emphasizing science as it is practiced by scientists rather than as a series of cookbook laboratory verifications of information previously known.
▲ Promote independent learning and analysis which engages the student in the design and conduct of the investigation.
▲ Increase emphasis on student ability to effectively communicate the results of their experiences.

A number of other papers (Deutch 1994; Gottfried et al., 1993; Wilson and Stensvold 1991; Seago 1992; Lawson 1992; and Leonard 1988, 1989, 1991), have focused specifically on college biology instruction and the effect of investigative laboratories on student performance, along with the development of critical thinking skills. An extraordinary degree of agreement is to be found among their recommendations, including the following:
▲ Students should be involved in the

design of their investigations and should make substantive decisions concerning its protocol and conduct including the option of making and correcting errors. Instructors should therefore provide only simple instructions and essential procedures and should resist telling the student how to carry out the investigation (Wilson and Stensvold 1991; Leonard 1991).
▲ The classroom and the laboratory should illustrate the nature of science and should introduce students to the thought processes and methods of science, such as formulating and testing of hypotheses, distinguishing between observations and inferences, controlling variables, and designing experiments (Gottfried et al., 1993).
▲ Students should have the opportunity of seeing how the process of science is linked to a mastery of basic techniques, and should have the chance to manipulate experimental materials and thus gain hands-on experience (Deutch 1994).
▲ Students should be expected to communicate the results of their investigations in a standard scientific format

(Seago 1992). This communication may be written, oral, or preferably both.

▲ Students should become familiar with the literature retrieval tools available at most college libraries (Seago 1992).

▲ Since research is time-consuming and somewhat uncertain, sufficient time should be allotted to the project to maximize the probability of success (Lawson 1992; Leonard 1988).

Of course, there are disadvantages to the investigative approach to laboratory teaching. Joyce and Weil (1992) acknowledge that

> students with a high need for structure were more uncomfortable with teaching strategies that provided low degrees of structure, whereas learners who preferred independent direction were more uncomfortable with teaching strategies that provided higher structure.

Some students will require more direction and encouragement, particularly in the early stages of their project than others. Nevertheless, Stewart (1988) found that in conducting student-designed laboratory experiments, students "come to class better prepared, are more careful in setting up the experiment, and are thus more interested in the result." But Stewart reports that the most intriguing aspect of such investigative laboratories is that there are "lots of surprises," and that these are the best inducements to learning and to experiencing the thrill of the scientific process.

We set out to design an investigative component of the laboratories of our general microbiology courses, which would embody the recommendations of previous studies. The intent was to develop an experience which would be challenging to students and which would engage them in limited but realistic research projects. This type of project has worked well in both of our institutions, one being a two-year campus of a large university, and the other a four-year liberal arts college. Each student or research team is expected to design and execute a semes-ter-length research project which requires them to isolate specific microorganisms from the environment. This task is embedded in and integrated with the normal course requirements.

METHOD

The projects have been phased to prevent student procrastination, and deadlines exist for submission of various parts of the project. This enables instructors to provide constructive feedback at the completion of each phase of the project. Slight differences in sequencing exist between our campuses, but that given here is representative. A scientific paper, in the format of the journal *Applied and Environmental Microbiology,* is required of all students at the end of the semester.

During the second week of the semester, a student or team of students randomly selects a card bearing the name of a specific organism or a class of organisms to be isolated. We refer to this as the "Organism to be Isolated" card. Examples of these appear in Table 1. Students may decide to work alone or in pairs. There are some limitations to this, as we point out later. The card drawn also has one reference dealing with the organism to be isolated. It is best that this not be the definitive reference on the subject, but should provide a starting point for students to approach the scientific literature. In addition to becoming familiar with various bibliographic search strategies, students learn to critically evaluate primary literature sources, in order to develop and execute workable isolation strategies.

By the fourth week the students must submit three additional references from the primary scientific literature. At least one working session is scheduled with a reference librarian to acquaint students with appropriate search strategies. These include the use of *Biological Abstracts, Biological and Agricultural Index, General Science Index,* and computer assisted techniques such as Info-Trac, Dialog, or CARL UNCOVER.

It has been our experience that it is very important for the course instructor to be present while library sessions are being conducted, for it reinforces the importance of the sessions and serves to eliminate any confusion about the search strategies or requirements. In many cases, the appropriate journals may not be found in the institution's library, so time needs to be allocated for interlibrary loans or for visits to other research libraries.

In the sixth lab week, students are required to submit three additional references on their organism, as well as a detailed outline of the proposed isolation protocol. Students are encouraged to develop their own procedures rather than merely use the methodology outlined in one of the references. The instructors provide feedback on the applicability of references and critique the isolation protocol. We do not attempt to impose any new methodology, but merely make an assessment of the feasibility of the proposed methodology. After the isolation protocol has been approved, the students must inventory the supplies and equipment that are needed. They become familiar with evaluating vendors, pricing, and the overall ordering process

While the library investigative work is proceeding, students are working in the laboratory becoming familiar with basic microbiological techniques. These include culture and transfer techniques, enumeration of microorganisms, microscopy, staining, nutrition and growth of organisms, media preparation, and sterilization techniques. Students work at mastering these techniques while they are collecting their references and formulating their own isolation procedures. By the eighth week, most students are ready to begin the actual laboratory work on their projects.

Since other laboratory exercises must also be completed during the semester, students must make judicious use of their time. The projects represent 20 to 25 percent of the students' final evaluation and constitute only a portion of the entire laboratory experience. Other traditional laboratory exercises such as Gram staining, use of selective and differential media, control of microbial growth, identification of organisms, and pathogenic microbiology experiments are completed during the course of the semester. In some cases students perform a series of investigative laboratories. These include the microbial characterization of an environment, the determination of optimal growth conditions for environmental isolates, experimental design for the determination of effectiveness of contact lens disinfectants, and examination of bactericidal properties of various hand soaps.

Students receive a copy of the "Instructions to Authors" section from the journal *Applied and Environmental Microbiology* (permission for use granted by the American Society for Microbiology). These instructions specify clearly the format to be used for the final research papers. At about the eighth week of the semester, a proposed introduction section of the paper is submitted for evaluation.

In weeks 10 and 12, students submit the "Materials and Methods" and the final Bibliography sections of the paper for review. The final paper, in *Applied and Environmental Microbiology* format, is turned in during the final week of the semester, along with a slant or plate of the isolated organism. The use of photomicrographs and microscope videotape sequences is encouraged.

In order for students to receive additional feedback prior to the submission of the final paper, one of us gives a mid-term assignment. Students must write a short, formal report on one of the investigative labs using the same format as the final research paper. This allows the instructor to critique the style of writing prior to the submission of the final paper.

The final papers are read twice: once, to evaluate the style and format, and the second time to judge the effort expended and to determine the quality of the lab work itself. Students are not penalized if they are unsuccessful in their isolation efforts. Emphasis

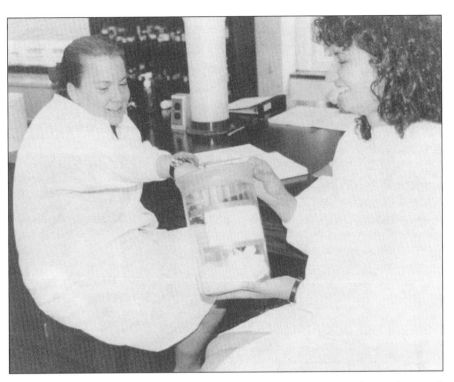

In the second week of their microbiology class, these Denison students select cards assigning them microorganisms to isolate in the laboratory over the course of the semester.

is placed upon effort, technique, and adherence to proper format.

If time permits, oral presentations and/or poster sessions of the research projects are presented to the class.

BENEFITS AND LIMITATIONS

The methodology described has been used with great success. Of course, there are both benefits and limitations to consider before adopting this type of format.

Benefits
▲ Students become familiar with experimental design, execution of experiments, and formal documentation of results. Too often these components are missing from introductory microbiology courses.
▲ The semester-length nature of the project fosters commitment by the students. They appreciate the timed nature of their assignments, and are not allowed to procrastinate before beginning their work.
▲ The project instills excitement. Students are more curious about the un-

certain aspects of the project as compared to known, standard "cookbook" exercises found in many laboratory manuals.
▲ Every student is required to prepare and sterilize media. Lab assistants are instructed to give suggestions, but each student or team must prepare all materials needed for the project.
▲ The project fosters collaboration among members of the team, and a healthy interaction occurs among all class members. Many students become curious about progress being made by other groups.
▲ Interestingly, the project has also encouraged students to broaden themselves in other aspects of the discipline of biology. For example, students attempting to isolate an organism from an invertebrate have consulted with zoology faculty for assistance, and have been encouraged to use information from other courses they have completed. In most situations, our faculty colleagues have been supportive and served as excellent resources.
▲ Students appreciate the relevance of

These Penn State students work with a reference librarian on a computerized search of the scientific literature.

many of the projects to "real world" problems, such as the isolation of bacteria from foods, or of organisms capable of degrading xenobiotic compounds.

▲ Students have an opportunity to improve their writing skills. Our approach fulfills many objectives of programs encouraging faculty to incorporate writing across the curriculum.

▲ In many cases, the student researchers decide to continue their projects in specific research courses, or are stimulated to embark on further research unrelated to the semester-length project.

Limitations

▲ The projects are time-consuming. Students should be aware of the extent of their commitment, which may involve lab hours outside of normal class

times.

▲ The coordination of projects and feedback given to students necessitates that this approach be used in courses where enrollments do not exceed 30 students.

▲ Students may find it difficult to make the decision to work alone or to work with a lab partner. In some cases the selected partner may be irresponsible in meeting deadlines, causing both members of the team to be penalized. Students should be cautioned in their selection of partners.

▲ Since students will need to use the laboratory in off hours, provision should be made to have supervisory personnel available for technical assistance and safety purposes.

▲ Instructors adopting this project approach may need to sacrifice some laboratory exercises in order to provide students sufficient time to work on

their projects during the scheduled laboratory hours.

▲ Depending on the projects selected and the reagents and media required, the cost of running the course may be higher than the traditional laboratory course.

▲ Due to the unpredictable nature of research, materials may need to be ordered on short notice. A good relationship with purchasing office personnel is helpful when this occurs.

▲ Some students are frustrated by their first experience in working independently on an open-ended project of this sort.

Student evaluations of the experience have been very positive. Some sample comments were:

"The project, although very frustrating at times, was very interesting and exciting. Doing your own research and experiments gave me a sense of worthiness and commitment."

"The project was interesting and helpful in improving my laboratory technique as well as encouraging research design and experimentation."

"The excitement and motivation helped me get through the long laboratory hours."

"Conducting the project left me better prepared than students who were in classes that did not conduct projects."

CONCLUSION

It has been our experience that the incorporation of a semester-length phased research project into our introductory microbiology courses promotes greater student interest and commitment to the class, as well as fostering independent learning of materials and skills. The project has its rewards and frustrations for both student and instructor. There are students who are accustomed to the "cookbook" style of laboratory exercise, and find the task confusing and intimidating, while others blossom in the free and challenging environment.

Typically, in a traditional course, cooperation among students in a learning environment is discouraged. However, in our approach cooperation is encouraged, and we often observe students making suggestions to one another, sharing references, and discussing their projects in a manner similar to the interplay that exists between researchers at a professional level. The final paper, written to a journal standard, is often the first that students have had to prepare, and provides a sense of pride and accomplishment for the students. The emphasis on citations and attribution serves as a valuable lesson in the avoidance of plagiarism.

Finally, each of us has received comments from returning students on the impact the project had in encouraging them to go into, or sometimes to avoid, research careers. ❏

Authors' Note
A complete list of successful projects, such as those enumerated in Table 1, may be obtained by writing to one of the authors.

Table 1. Examples of semester-length research projects.

A bacterial virus.
Reference: Farrah, Samuel R. 1987. "Ecology of Phage in Freshwater Environments." In Goyal, S.M. et al. *Phage Ecology,* pp. 125-136. New York: John Wiley and Sons.

An oligotrophic microorganism.
Reference: Fry, J.C. 1990. "Oligotrophs." In Edwards, Clive, ed. *Microbiology of Extreme Environments,* pp. 93-116. New York: McGraw-Hill, New York.

A microbial contaminant in a pharmaceutical, cosmetic, or toiletry product.
Reference: Baird, R.M. 1988. "Microbiological Contamination of Manufactured Products: Official and Unofficial Limits." In Bloomfield, S.F., et al., ed. *Microbial Quality Assurance in Pharmaceuticals, Cosmetics and Toiletries,* pp. 61-76. Halsted Press, New York.

Organism capable of degrading EDTA.
Reference: Nortemann, Bernd. 1992. "Total Degradation of EDTA by Mixed Cultures and a Bacterial Isolate." *Applied and Environmental Microbiology* 58: 671-676.

References

Aaronson, S. 1970. *Experimental Microbial Ecology.* New York: Academic Press.

Ainsworth, G.C. and A.S. Sussman. 1965. *The Fungi: An Advanced Treatise.* New York: Academic Press.

American Association for the Advancement of Science. 1989. *Project 2061: Science For All Americans.* Washington, D.C.: AAAS.

American Association for the Advancement of Science. 1990. *The Liberal Art of Science: Agenda For Action.* Washington, D.C.: AAAS.

American Association for the Advancement of Science. 1993. *Benchmarks For Science Literacy: Project 2061.* Washington, D.C.: AAAS.

Annual Review of Microbiology. Annual volumes since 1946. Palo Alto, Ca.: Annual Reviews Inc.

Atlas, Ronald M. 1993. *Handbook of Microbiological Media.* Boca Raton, Fla.: CRC Press.

Atlas, R.M. and R. Bartha. 1993. *Microbial Ecology: Fundamentals and Applications.* 3d ed. Menlo Park, Ca.: Benjamin/Cummings.

Austin, B., ed. 1988. *Methods in Aquatic Bacteriology.* New York: John Wiley and Sons.

Bergey's Manual of Systematic Bacteriology, 1984-1989. Baltimore, Md.: Williams and Wilkins.

Cannon, Robert E. 1990. Experiments with writing to teach microbiology." *The American Biology Teacher* 52: 156-158.

Deutch, Charles E. 1994. Restructuring a general microbiology laboratory into an investigative experience. *The American Biology Teacher* 56: 294-296.

Difco Manual. 10th ed. 1984. Detroit, Mi.: Difco Laboratories.

Gerhardt, P., R.G.E. Murray, W.A. Wood, and N.R. Krieg, eds. 1993. *Methods for General and Molecular Bacteriology.* Washington, D.C.: American Society for Microbiology.

Gottfried, Sandra, Rita Hoots, Robert Creek, Raymond Tamppari, Thomas Lord, and Rae Ann Sines. 1993. College biology teaching: a literature review, recommendations and a research agenda. *The American Biology Teacher* 55: 340-348.

Holt, J.G., N.R. Krieg, P.H.A. Sneath, J.T. Staley, and S.T. Williams, eds. 1994. *Bergey's Manual of Determinative Bacteriology,* 9th ed. Baltimore, Md.: Williams and Wilkins.

Joyce, Bruce and Marsha Weil with Beverly Showers. 1992. *Models of Teaching,* 4th ed. Allyn and Bacon.

Klug, M.J. and C.A. Reddy. eds. 1984. *Current Perspectives in Microbial Ecology.* Washington, D.C.: American Society for Microbiology.

Labeda, D.P., ed. 1990. *Isolation of Biotechnological Organisms from Nature.* New York: McGraw-Hill.

Lawson, Anton E. 1992. The development of reasoning among college biology students-a review of research. *Journal of College Science Teaching* 21: 338-344.

Leonard, William H. 1988. An experimental test of an extended dissection laboratory approach for university general biology. *Journal of Research in Science Teaching* 26: 79-91.

Leonard, William H. 1989. Ten years of research on investigative laboratory instruction strategies. *Journal of College Science Teaching* 18: 304-306.

Leonard, William H. 1991. A recipe for "uncookbooking" laboratory investigations. *Journal of College Science Teaching* 21: 84-87.

Lederberg, J. 1992. *Encyclopedia of Microbiology.* San Diego, Ca.: Academic Press.

Moore, Randy. 1993. Does writing about science improve learning about science? *Journal of College Science Teaching* 22: 212-217.

National Research Council. 1990. *Fulfilling the Promise: Biology Education in the Nation's Schools.* Washington, D.C.: National Academy of Sciences Press.

O'Leary, William M. 1989. *Practical Handbook of Microbiology.* Boca Raton, Fla.: CRC Press, Inc.

Poindexter, J.S. and E.R. Leadbetter. 1986. *Bacteria in Nature.* New York: Plenum.

Rodina, E.G. 1972. *Methods in Aquatic Microbiology.* Baltimore, Md.: University Press.

Seago, James L, Jr. 1992. The role of research in undergraduate instruction. *The American Biology Teacher* 54: 401-405.

Standard Methods for the Examination of Water and Wastewater. 14th ed. 1975. Washington, D.C.: American Public Health Association.

Stewart, Barbara Y. 1988. The surprise element of a student-designed laboratory experiment. *Journal of College Science Teaching* 17: 269-273.

Stolf, H. 1988. *Microbial Ecology: Organisms, Habitats, Activities.* New York: Cambridge University Press.

Walker, N. 1975. *Soil Microbiology.* New York: John Wiley and Sons.

Wilson, John T. and Mark S. Stensvold. 1991. Improving instruction: an interpretation of research. *Journal of College Science Teaching* 20: 350-353.

Old Wine into New Bottles

How Traditional Lab Exercises Can Be Converted into Investigative Ones

G. Douglas Crandall

In the past several years, I have become increasingly aware of a trend in biology laboratories that encourages a move away from the more traditional method of teaching (demonstration-observation) toward a more investigative one. The object of this newer, more analytical approach is to teach not only the facts of science but also the process of science.

In 1969, Holt et al. made the first call for investigative or inquiry-based lab instruction, and since then a growing number of articles dedicated to some aspect of this approach have followed.

The "Science As A Way Of Knowing" series in the *American Zoologist* (1984-1989) is a detailed and broadly based response to this call providing a rich source of information in a variety of biological disciplines. Others have made their contribution with specific applications of the approach to individual courses (Heady 1993; Bozzone 1994; Sundberg and Moncada 1994).

Yet other researchers have developed testing procedures to assess the extent to which students have acquired the process skills associated with scientific reasoning and problem solving (Dillashaw and Okey 1980; Tobin and Capie 1982; Burns, Okey, and Wise 1985). In addition, at least one major publisher has supported investigative methods through the publication of a lab manual with both traditional and open-ended investigative exercises (Morgan and Carter 1993).

G. Douglas Crandall is an associate professor of biology, Emmanuel College, 400 The Fenway, Boston, MA 02115.

I was especially impressed by Lawson's review article (1992) that suggests that investigative labs improve student problem-solving skills with no decrease in overall content acquisition, and as a special bonus...the students enjoy it more! The difference now appears to be that, in addition to the educators, the foundations and publishers are interested in making special efforts to support teacher workshops and promulgate materials designed with inquiry-based learning as its goal.

During the summer of 1993, I had the good fortune to participate in LABSHOP, an NSF sponsored workshop at Illinois State University that emphasized the design of investigative lab exercises for introductory biology courses. The forty-plus participants included biology faculty from all over the country who teach these introductory labs. The participants were divided into nine groups by topic (natural selection, cytology, respiration, etc.) and instructed to design and pilot an investigative lab exercise suitable for introductory courses. The lab exercises that resulted from this effort were posted on an electronic bulletin board (BIOLAB) and are now available through the world wide web.

As the LABSHOP participants deliberated throughout that week, two critical points became abundantly clear:
▲ not all lab exercises are equally well suited to the method;
▲ investigative labs are more time consuming than traditional ones.

Some exercises lend themselves very nicely to the investigative approach. Our group developed lab exercises on cell division and membrane transport.

After a day of brainstorming several approaches to these exercises, we agreed that it was pretty easy to think of transport experiments that could be presented in an investigative manner but that cell division presented some real problems.

One discovery we made is that all techniques and procedures are not equally adaptable to the investigative format. Procedures that are simple, experimental, easily learned, and provide meaningful results are the best. For example, an exercise demonstrating osmosis with sugar solutions and dialysis tubing fulfills all of these criteria. However, the techniques required to investigate cell division do not readily meet these requirements. Considering the time constraints of a one week workshop, our group decided to work on an osmosis exercise rather than cell division.

By its very nature this way of teaching is time consuming. The instructor should plan at least twice as much time for an investigative lab to allow for discussion and experimental design. A traditional transport lab at the introductory level might, in a single session, demonstrate diffusion, osmosis, and several aspects of cellular transport. An investigative lab based upon the osmosis component alone requires two lab sessions. The first lab consists of a prelab discussion, a preliminary trial of experimental methods followed by discussion of results, and time for the students to design their own experiments. During the entire second session, students execute their own experiments and discuss results. Note that much of the burden of planning that is ordinarily done by the instructor (before

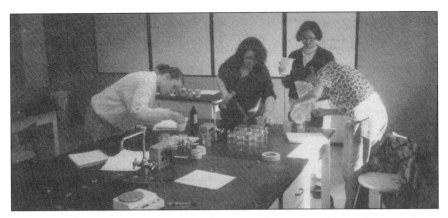
After planning their experiment, a student research group works together to set it up.

the lab) is now borne by the students (during the lab).

Critics of this methodology might point out that with increased time set aside for investigative labs, some content might be lost. If it takes two weeks to investigate osmosis compared with one week to be exposed to all aspects of cellular transport something is lost. Ultimately the important difference is expressed in the verbs *investigate and expose*. Will they learn more biology from the *investigation* of a process or by being *exposed* to it? I think we all know the answer.

If we want our introductory students to *learn the facts of biology and the process of science*, we must develop a sequence of lab exercises with an appropriate balance of traditional and investigative labs. The exact ratio will vary. Some have adopted the view that content is covered in the lecture and process in the lab, in which case the lab can be completely investigative. Although this approach may be appropriate for upper-level courses (Heady 1993), it is less suitable for an introductory course. If you are new to this approach, you might start by introducing a single investigative lab each semester, evaluate the results, and as you and the students become more comfortable with it add exercises as appropriate. Your final mix of traditional and investigative labs will vary depending upon the level of your students, time availability, and your own inclination to experiment with this method.

An effective approach to selecting

this is to examine the lab exercises that match your present offerings in the introductory course and choose **one** that looks like it would be easily converted to an investigative lab. Good candidates for conversion:
▲ require methods that can be easily and quickly demonstrated to the students;
▲ produce meaningful data in a relatively short period of time.

I have done the following lab exercise on seed germination in a traditional manner for many years. Recently, I have used the same basic protocol but scheduled more time and let students design their own experiments based upon their initial results. I present this as *an example of a traditional lab that was easily converted to an investigative one*. The obvious advantage of this approach is that students not only learn the basic requirements for seed germination, but also have an opportunity to design their own experiments to further explore the phenomenon. On the negative side, this lab now takes three sessions as compared to two previously:
▲ Week 1: prelab discussion, preliminary trial
▲ Week 2: collection of data from preliminary trial, discussion of results, and design of individual experiments
▲ Week 3: execution of experiments, discussion of data collection, and presentation.

PRELAB DISCUSSION

During the first lab, I begin with an open-ended discussion probing the students' understanding of seed germi-

nation. We talk about what happens to seeds during the early stages of a plant's existence and the conditions necessary to initiate and support the process. As new terms arise, I write them on the board and encourage students to define them. Where necessary I fill in the gaps. Eventually, the students understand that the fundamental ingredients for seeds to germinate are moisture, appropriate temperatures, and oxygen. Rather than stop there, I challenge them to suggest ways they might demonstrate the veracity of this conclusion. At this point in the discussion, I accept just about anything they suggest in order to keep ideas flowing.

When the free discussion begins to flag, I structure the discussion more and talk about realistic experimental design. Certain experiments are just frivolous and would yield little useful information (e.g., will seeds germinate in beer?). We talk about controlled experiments that are designed to show the impact of a single factor at a time. I stress the importance of designing experiments that do not ask too many questions simultaneously. Finally, I tell the students about the week-long exercise that will begin that day, which is designed to illustrate the importance of air, water, and temperature on seed germination, and stress that it will give them the tools to design additional experiments in the future.

PRELIMINARY TRIAL

The exercise described below requires that student groups set up four germination chambers. I typically have 15-20 students in the lab and divide them into collaborative groups of three to five each. In the control chamber, conditions are ideal for germination (adequate moisture, air, and moderate temperatures). The conditions in the remaining experimental chambers are identical except that a single factor is missing or limited. After one week of observations the chambers are dismantled and each of the experimental groups compared with the control. This exercise yields excellent qualitative and quantitative information regarding the requirements for seed germination.

Students prepare germination chambers to test the effect of different environmental conditions on the germination of pea seeds.

DESIGN OF INDEPENDENT STUDENT EXPERIMENTS

Once all of the data are collected, I allow time for exchange of results and discussion. We spend a lot of time during this second session comparing data, talking about how conclusions are drawn from results, and how the experimental design could be improved. I then remind the students that the following week they will be doing their own independently designed experiments on seed germination. I challenge them as individual lab groups to brainstorm and design an experiment. They should plan to use basically the same methods and materials but in different ways to delve further into the germination process. For example, the first exercise clearly shows that water is required for germination, but *how much* water is needed? Initially, I let them work on their own to develop a basic plan, then act as a resource to help them refine the experiment so that it is both possible and practical.

During the brainstorming period, I continue to develop the student's understanding of experimental design and reinforce the use of relevant terminology. I encourage them to form an *hypothesis* and phrase it as an *"If...then" statement* that should enable them to design an experiment that will test the hypothesis. For example: "If the seeds are exposed to incrementally larger amounts of water then they will germinate more quickly."

I ask them many questions to be sure that they are moving toward a reasonable experimental design. How will they administer different amounts of water to the seeds? How do they plan to measure the response of the seeds to the varying amounts of water? I talk to them about the different types of *variables* in such an experiment (controlled, dependent, and independent). I use the more descriptive terms, *manipulated variable* for independent variable and *responding variable* for dependent variable (Burns, Okey, and Wise 1985).

In the proposed experiment, the con-trolled variables are the same in each germination chamber (temperature, light, etc.), while the amount of water added to each experimental chamber represents the manipulated variable and the changes in seedling growth represent the responding variable.

It is important to point out that student-designed experiments will not be of Nobel Prize-winning caliber. In fact, it is most likely that they will be pretty crude. However, as students go through this process they learn and get better, so if this is their first time through, do not be disappointed. The idea is to encourage a simple, sound plan with prospects of success. Examples of my own students' experiments include investigation of the effect of the following factors on germination:

▲ different germination temperatures
▲ storing seeds at different temperatures prior to germination
▲ different pHs
▲ different salt (NaCl) concentrations
▲ light
▲ different amounts of water
▲ a partial vacuum

At the end of this discussion I collect a proposal from each student group. The proposal should clearly state their hypothesis, experimental design, and a list of materials necessary for running the experiment. This ensures that I will have all the necessary materials ready for the following week. To ensure consis-

After one week, the germination chambers are dismantled and the seedlings weighed and measured.

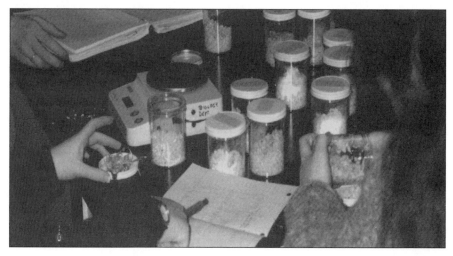

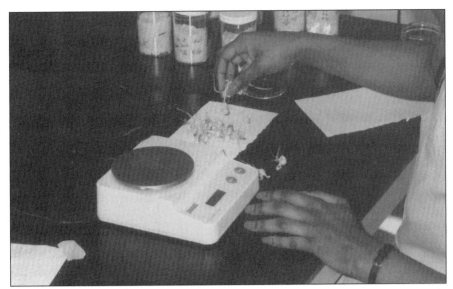

Seedlings are weighed before and after germination to determine percent weight change.

tency, I have developed a standardized form for the proposal.

During the third lab session, the students set up their own experiments. I use any extra time for the groups to share their experimental designs and expected results. This is also a good time to talk with the groups about how their data are to be collected, processed, and presented. Will they do statistical analysis of the data? Should the data be presented in tables and/or graphs? Finally, let the students know in what form the final product of their work should be: a lab report, research paper, oral presentation, or poster session. It is also important to emphasize that this is an independent project and that they are responsible for all data collection on their own time. I have found that students accustomed to the traditional lab find it difficult to think in terms of coming to the lab at any other time than the scheduled period.

SEED GERMINATION REQUIREMENTS
Student Protocol

The protocol for the seed germination lab is identical to its previous use as a traditional, noninvestigative lab.

1. Prepare four germination chambers
a. Select four containers and identify them with your initials and the date. Label the chambers as follows:
  A. Control

  B. No Air
  C. No Water
  D. Low Temperature
b. Line the bottom of each chamber with a layer of absorbent cotton about 1 cm thick (Schroeder 1995) reports that a similar depth of perlite works equally well).
c. Thoroughly moisten the cotton in containers A, B, and D. Once the water has soaked in pour off the excess.
d. Count out 25 pea seeds and determine their total weight to the nearest tenth of a gram. Repeat this process three more times so that you have four groups of 25 seeds each. Record the weight data in your notebook.
e. Scatter 25 pea seeds over the cotton in each germination chamber. Distribute the seeds so that there is uniform contact between the seeds and the cotton.
f. Loosely cover containers A, C, and D. This can be accomplished with a loose plug of dry cotton or by partially screwing the lid on a screw-top jar. Whichever way this is done, it is important that there be exchange of air between the inside of the container and the atmosphere with a minimum of evaporation.

2. Special conditions as indicated in *Table 1* should be maintained for one week.
Control—leave this chamber at room temperature (~20° C), seeds in this

container will have ample moisture and oxygen, and sufficiently warm temperatures to ensure normal germination.
No Air—the lid on this jar should be tightly closed and sealed with a strip of Parafilm and/or tape. Place this airtight container with the control.
No Water—place this chamber with the control.
Low Temperature—place this container in the refrigerator (~5° C).

3. Observations and Discussion
a. For one week, make daily observations comparing the events in the Control Chamber with each of the experimental chambers. Record the results (measurements, drawings, etc.) in your note book. Determine when and if germination occurs, the appearance of the seedlings, etc. What is the first sign of germination? When does germination begin? Describe the sequence of events during the first week of germination.
b. At the end of one week, dismantle the germination chambers and carefully separate the cotton from the seedlings. Count the number of germinated and ungerminated seeds in each chamber and calculate the percent germination (Equation 1). Record the results in **Table 2**.

$$(1)\ \%\ \text{Germination} = \frac{\#\ \text{of Germinated Seeds}}{\text{Total}\ \#\ \text{of Seeds}} \times 100$$

Blot the seedlings dry with paper toweling and determine the total weight of the seedlings in each container. Compare these results with the dry weight of the seeds at the beginning of the experiment. Calculate the percent weight gain or loss (Equations 2 and 3) and record the results in **Table 3**.

$$(2)\ \text{Percent Gain} = \frac{\text{Increase in Weight}}{\text{Initial Weight}} \times 100$$

$$(3)\ \text{Percent Loss} = \frac{\text{Decrease in Weight}}{\text{Initial Weight}} \times 100$$

Describe the extent of germination under each set of conditions in a qualitative way, *i.e.* Have the seeds swollen? Produced roots? Leaves? What is the color and size of plant parts? Measure the length of roots, leaves, and stems of all seedlings in each chamber. Report the average for each set of conditions in **Table 4**.

c. Lab Report

Prepare a combined table of results which illustrates, by experimental condition: percent germination, percent weight gain or loss, average length of roots, stems, and leaves.

Of the factors tested, which is the most critical to germination? Support your answer with data and list the other factors in descending order of importance.

Based upon the conditions in chamber B (No Air), what can you actually conclude about the necessity of air to germination? Discuss how this part of the experiment could be improved to truly show the necessity of air (oxygen).

Most seeds do not require light for germination. Does this experiment give any information about the necessity of light for germination? Describe how you might set up an experiment to test for the necessity of light in seed germination.

Have the ungerminated seeds been permanently damaged? What could you do to determine whether these seeds can still germinate?

MATERIALS

The following list of materials assumes a lab section of 20 students divided into five groups of four each.
▲ Germination chambers (20)—wide-mouth, screw-top plastic jars with a volume equal to 200-300 ml work the best, but other containers will also serve. Large test tubes, baby food jars, plastic food containers, etc. will all do fine. The critical features are that the containers must be *clear* so that the germination process can be readily observed and *wide-mouthed* so the contents can be easily removed at the end of the experiment.
▲ One box of absorbent cotton (1 ounce)
▲ Marking tape (5 rolls) and marking pens (5)

Table 1. Conditions in Each Germination Chamber

Chamber	Conditions	Water	Air	Temperature
A	Control	+	+	~20 C
B	No Air	+	-	~20 C
C	No Water	-	+	~20 C
D	Low Temp	+	+	~5 C

Table 2. Percent Seed Germination in Each Chamber

Chamber	Conditions	Number Germinated	Number Ungerminated	Percent Germinated
A	Control			
B	No Air			
C	No Water			
D	Low Temp			

Table 3. Weight Gain or Loss by Seedlings

Chamber	Conditions	Initial Weight (g)	Final Weight (g)	Difference Gain (+) Loss (-)	Percent Change (+/-)
A	Control				
B	No Air				
C	No Water				
D	Low Temp				

Table 4. Size changes in seedlings

Chamber	Conditions	Average length (cm)		
		Leaves	Roots	Stems
A	Control			
B	No Air			
C	No Water			
D	Low Temp			

▲ Dry seeds (600)-Pea seeds are ideal because they are big and germinate quickly, but other seeds (radish, bean, corn) work very well.
▲ Triplebeam or similar balance to weigh seeds before and after the experiment. If each group has its own balance the exercise goes much more quickly.
▲ Paper toweling (1 roll)
▲ Centimeter ruler (10)
▲ Tap water (1 liter)
▲ Refrigerator—if a refrigerator is not available, set up a styrofoam cooler with ice and replenish the ice on a daily basis. The temperature should be maintained around 0-5° C.
▲ Parafilm (1 roll) and scissors

DISCUSSION

My initial aim in using the investigative teaching approach was to involve students more intimately in the scientific process and to let them experience the joys and disappointments of experimental work. I wanted them to learn the language of experimental design, to understand through their own experiences how an experiment is designed, carried out, and interpreted. A secondary goal was to make the laboratory component of the course more enjoyable.

Student evaluation forms filled out by 35 of 46 students after completion of the project indicated that I was able to achieve the above goals. When I asked: "The aim of this project was to involve you in the *process* of a scientific investigation. To what extent do you feel that this was accomplished?", 27 responded that the goal was reached, two that it was not, and the remaining six gave no response. When I asked if they had a: "better/worse/no change idea of what is involved in planning and carrying out a scientific investigation," 29 responded better, one worse, and the remainder felt there was no change (three) or did not respond (two). Finally, when I asked if they: "enjoyed, hated, or had no special reaction to the experience," 26 responded that they enjoyed the project, one hated it, and the remaining eight had no special reaction to the project.

Students reported that they liked being able to share the responsibility of planning and carrying out the experiments with others, supporting an hypothesis with data, and "having the trust and respect from the professor that we could do it." Others indicated that, although the experience was a good one, it was stressful, time consuming, and not always appropriate. Although negative responses were few, one student felt that not everyone in her group took it seriously and this detracted from the final result. When asked if they would like *all* lab exercises to be inquiry based, the results were mixed: about one-third of the students thought that it would be a good idea, another third were opposed, and the remainder thought that a mix of investigative and traditional labs was preferable. This variation reflects the experience of Sundberg and Moncada (1994) who, in assessing student attitudes toward investigative labs, found that their impact was as likely to be negative as positive.

I am greatly encouraged by these responses and plan to introduce more investigative lab experiences in all of my courses. I also plan to begin testing students before and after the course to determine whether there is improvement in reasoning skills and scientific thought.

The protocol I have described is basically the same for a traditional lab or an investigative one. The major difference lies in the presentation, time, and degree of student involvement. The single most important ingredient in a successful inquiry-based lab is *active* student involvement. Once the students begin to have "ownership" of their lab work, their level of interest and involvement significantly increases.

This is a good example of how the transition from noninvestigative labs to investigative ones can be made. An instructor does not necessarily need to begin from scratch inventing new lab exercises, but can go back to many of the old standards and convert them with a minimum of effort. The biggest difference between traditional labs and inquiry-based ones lies in the *presenta-*

tion. A successful exercise begins with a good strong prelab introducing students to the scientific process, injecting lots of dialog throughout, and including a sense of student ownership in the project.

Experience indicates that not *all* lab exercises can or should be taught using the investigative approach. Some are just too time consuming while others are just not practically amenable to the approach. As you examine your present traditional lab exercises for possible candidates, look for those that: (1) have an experimental approach; (2) involve techniques that are easily taught and mastered; and (3) provide dependable, reproducible results. □

Note
Interested parties may obtain additional information about the BIOLAB bulletin board and home page from Dr. Joseph E. Armstrong <jearmstr@ilstu.edu> or Dr. Marshall D.Sundberg <sundberg@life. jsc.nasa.gov> who function as the BIOLAB systems operators. Dr. Armstrong is Professor of Biology at Illinois State University and Dr. Sundberg is Associate Professor of Plant Biology at Louisiana State University.

Acknowledgements
The author would like to extend his sincere thanks to Joseph Armstrong, Marshall Sundberg, and Doreen Schroeder whose careful reading of an earlier draft of this manuscript was extremely helpful.

References
Bozzone, D. M. 1994. An experimental system to study cell differentiation. *Journal of College Science Teaching* 23(6): 363-366.

Burns, J. C., J. R. Okey, and K. Wise. 1985. Development of an integrated process skill test: TIPS II. *Journal of Research in Science Teaching* 22(2): 169-177.

Dillashaw, G. F., and J. R. Okey. 1980. Test of the integrated science process skills for secondary science students. *Science Education* 64(5): 601-608.

Heady, J. E. 1993. Teaching embryology without lectures and without traditional laboratories—An adventure in innovation. *Journal of College Science Teaching* 23(2): 87-91.

Holt, C. E., P. Abramoff, L. V. Wilcox, and D. L. Abell. 1969. Investigative laboratory programs in biology. *Bioscience* 19(12): 1104-1107.

Lawson, A. E. 1992. The development of reasoning among college biology students—A review of research. *Journal of College Science Teaching* 21(6): 338-344.

Morgan, J. G., and M. E. Carter. 1993. *Investigating Biology: A Laboratory Manual for BIOLOGY.* Redwood City, CA: Benjamin/Cummings Publishing Co., Inc.

Schroeder, D. 1995. personal communication.

Sundberg, M. D., and G. J. Moncada. 1994. Creating effective investigative laboratories for undergraduates. *BioScience* 44(10): 698-704.

Tobin, K. G., and W. Capie. 1982. Development and validation of a group test of integrated processes. *Journal of Research in Science Teaching* 19(2): 133-141.

Semester-Length Field Investigations in Undergraduate Animal Behavior and Ecology Courses

Making the Laboratory Experience the Linchpin of Science Education

Jeffrey D. Weld, Christopher M. Rogers, and Stephen B. Heard

Undergraduate science laboratory courses often use "cookbook" exercises where expected results are known without the need for thought or experiment. The University of Iowa's elective courses Animal Behavior and Ecology provide authentic field study experience for undergraduates using hypothetico-deductive methodology (hypotheses and predictions), experimental design and interpretation, and collaboration, resulting in a scientific paper.

Collegiate science education is faced with a dilemma: the skills and experience gained through laboratory science are recognized as a practical necessity for the well-being of individuals and society, yet administrative and budgetary constraints in colleges and universities are undercutting this vital dimension of undergraduate education.

The Commission on Undergraduate Education in the Biological Sciences recommended the adoption of a strong investigative lab component for undergraduate science courses in that body's 1971 report (Thornton 1971). Twenty-six years later, the

National Science Foundation (NSF) continues to promote a widely unheeded call for bolstering the laboratory component of undergraduate science for the sake of a future that "... will increasingly require that citizens have a substantial understanding of the methods and content of science and technology—and some understanding of their potential and limitations as well as their interconnectedness" (NSF 1996).

A RATIONALE FOR CHANGE

The importance of undergraduate lab science is underscored by findings that identify introductory science courses at the freshman and sophomore years as a crucial link in the chain influencing an undergraduate's decision to major in science (Merriam 1988).

Moreover, the NSF identifies undergraduate science education as "the linchpin of the entire [science education] enterprise—for it is at the undergraduate level that prospective K-12 teachers are educated, that most of the technical workforce is prepared, and that future educators and professional practi-

tioners...learn their fields" (NSF 1996).

In their review of the research on benefits of laboratory investigation, Lazarowitz and Tamir (1994) identified five intellectual gains made by students across studies. Laboratory science provides students the chance to:

▲ identify and rectify misconceptions that would likely persist in more didactic science experiences;

▲ develop their inquiry and intellectual skills, and appreciate the spirit and nature of science;

▲ develop cognitive abilities such as problem solving, analysis, critical

Jeffrey D. Weld is an assistant professor of science education at Oklahoma State University, 245 Willard Hall, Stillwater, OK 74078; e-mail: jweld@ okstate.edu. Christopher M. Rogers is an assistant professor of zoology, Grinnell College, Grinnell, IA 50112; at the writing of this article he was an adjunct assistant professor at the University of Iowa. Stephen B. Heard is an assistant professor of ecology, (W)318 Chemistry-Botany Building, University of Iowa, Iowa City, IA 52242.

thinking, synthesis, evaluation, and creativity;

▲ develop attributes such as honesty, readiness to admit failure, critical assessment of results and their limitations, curiosity, risk taking, precision, perseverance, collaboration, and readiness to work toward consensus;

▲ enjoy practical and nontrivial work in the laboratory, which in turn fosters motivation and interest in pursuing study in science (Lazarowitz and Tamir 1994).

Although universal consensus exists for valuing these skills and attributes in every citizen, many science programs are falling short of their realization in undergraduate science coursework. Between 1964 and 1993, the percentage of colleges and universities with an undergraduate natural science requirement that included some form of laboratory work declined from 80 to 30 percent (Moore 1996). From 1970 to 1980 alone, laboratory courses offered and taken by undergraduates in America's colleges dropped by 20 percent (NSF 1996).

This trend led to a scathing 1986 report from the National Science Board that cited laboratory instruction "which has deteriorated to the point where it is often uninspired, tedious, and dull. Too frequently it is conducted in facilities and with instruments that are obsolete and inadequate....It is also being eliminated from many introductory courses" (National Science Board 1986).

Two pressures have driven this decline (NSF 1996). First, average class size has crept upward at four percent per year from 1979 to 1989. Second, despite an average rise in tuition rates of 25 percent from 1980 to 1992, the cost per student as educational input has risen even faster. The net result—more students and less financial support has stretched budgets for equipment, laboratory facilities, and faculty development. Many institutions, therefore, have made decisions to lower overall costs by reducing the

number of lab sections and adding or substituting nonlaboratory courses (NSF 1996).

To reverse this trend, colleges must address budget concerns for lab science, increase student enrollment in lab science, and base laboratory instructional methods on current learning research. More undergraduate laboratory courses are needed that operate on a modest budget, accommodate increasing numbers of students

A student places monitoring equipment in a pond to measure algal growth as part of a field project on top-down trophic control in ecology.

without draining inordinate time and energy from instructors, and incorporate true scientific inquiry.

The undergraduate elective courses, Animal Behavior and Ecology at the University of Iowa, together fulfill these needs through semester-length field investigations. The independent nature of the work allows more flexibility and less integral involvement on a daily basis for the instructors, and the structure (or intentional lack thereof) of the investigations reflects real science, complete with unknown and potentially meaningful outcomes. Finally,

the cost is negligible compared to more traditional lab courses.

METHODOLOGY

Animal Behavior and Ecology are both undergraduate elective courses. Each has a large lecture section (80 students) supplemented by multiple lab sections (20 students). Lecture section size should have no negative impact on the field investigations so long as adequate teaching assistant (TA) support exists along with adequate field sites.

No definitive student profile exists for either course; enrollees represent virtually every academic major at every level of study, from freshman to senior to graduate student. The discussion component of the two courses was replaced by the current semester-length field studies developed by one of us (CMR) at the University of Iowa in 1992.

At the first weekly meeting of the lab section, students are introduced to the field studies. Three or four tractable behavioral or ecological questions and hypotheses are presented by the instructor (examples of these topics are listed in **Table 1**).

The initial discussion presents a) background information on each question, including natural history, ecology, taxonomy, and potential hypotheses, b) logistical considerations unique to each topic (e.g., the locations of local public woodlands or ponds to be used as study sites), and c) goals and expectations for the lab, including deadlines, teaming options, and the format of a final write-up. Students then elect to sign up for one of the investigative topics.

Students are assembled into teams of four to five members by virtue of their choice of study. Teams are then responsible for generating predictions that lead to experimental design. At the mandatory second weekly meeting, teams meet to outline their plan for investigation with close collaboration of the lab instructor.

Teams must delegate tasks and

devise a schedule. Instructors provide the necessary equipment, as well as varying degrees of design and resource assistance. Most subsequent sessions are devoted to independent research. Instructors continue to be on hand during scheduled lab sessions for teams who may need consultation, but attendance at these sessions is not required.

Typically, one or two of five teams from each section may "drop in" during each session, generally for advice on unforeseen difficulties with an experimental design, for help interpreting emerging findings and with statistical analysis and formatting of the paper, and for assistance on locating relevant literature.

One more mandatory lab is scheduled one-third of the way through the semester, where students present a one-page progress report. This allows the instructor a final check on the quality and tractability of each experimental design. Actual time spent in the field has averaged 25 to over 40 hours per student over the duration of an investigation. Example studies are described in **Tables 2 and 3**.

To ensure that the research conducted by the students bears on a current question or hypothesis in ecology or animal behavior, students are required to generate a report in the form of a scientific paper formatted for the journals *Ecology* or *Animal Behaviour*. Papers include an introduction where students must place their research question in a context of past work, a detailed description of methods and materials, a report of results with tables and/or graphs and statistical analysis, a discussion that compares their findings to initial hypotheses and the findings of others, and a list of the literature cited in the work (a minimum of five references is required).

Instructors provide the service of data review, experimental critique, and statistical consultation throughout the semester at the optional "drop-in" weekly discussion sessions. This practice diminishes anxiety on the part of students who, in the absence of the detailed lab instructions to which they are accustomed, sometimes wonder if they are "on the right track." The research paper comprises 25 percent of the course grade.

BENEFITS AND LIMITATIONS TO FIELD PROJECTS

Although student evaluations of the field studies have been largely positive (sample comments follow), inevitable trade-offs exist in terms of the implementation and evaluation of this style of laboratory.

Benefits

Field studies are real science. The investigations are of current topics of research and results are unknown in advance. Rather than following a "cookbook" procedure, students are given a general problem and some suggestions, but must develop their own hypotheses and predictions and design and carry out their own experiments and observations. They must define appropriate statistical approaches ahead of time, establish random sampling procedures, and adjust procedures when problems crop up.

Field studies in Animal Behavior and Ecology mirror the real world in that they involve hard work, bad weather, complicated data, and unpredictable events (such as road crews mowing down goldenrod halfway through an experiment). Field studies also foster responsibility in students, who must organize time, delegate responsibility, plan and think ahead, and contribute to a final product.

The strength of teaming enables each member—freshman through graduate student—to bring particular expertise in writing, statistics, and experimental design to the investigation.

Field studies are enjoyable for students. At the close of each semester, students are anonymously queried about the field studies. Of the 65 most recent surveys, 61 were positive with regard to field studies. In answer to the question "How useful and interesting did you find the field project, compared to other biology labs you've taken?" representative comments include:

▲ This was so much more useful in comparison to other labs. You learn from other people in the lab, and you get to invent an experiment instead of read about it.

▲ The projects were very informational and gave me an idea of things an ecologist does. It is more interesting.

▲ I enjoyed the field project because it was different and applicable because we did the entire experiment on our own. Most labs you read a text and follow instructions and get nothing out of them.

Occasional comments attest to the value of authentic investigations in attracting new scientists:

▲ It was interesting to do a field lab (my first)—reinforces my interest in the biological sciences.

▲ I absolutely loved it. I plan on being a field biologist and this was my first true field experience.

The cost of field studies is favorable compared to a more traditional laboratory format. Average cost per student over the three years of implementation for Animal Behavior and Ecology is seven dollars. The materials necessary to run field investigations are under the creative control of the instructor who can guide experimental design, assuring that needs do not get too elaborate.

Common purchases include bricks, eggs, plastic owl models, thermometers, bird seed, and fishing line. Some existing equipment, such as balances and spectrophotometers, are used in some projects for short periods; these should be available in most biology departments.

Limitations

Fair grading of a group product can be problematic, particularly when differential effort occurs among group members. Two instances have arisen out of over one hundred projects to date in which students registered complaints with the instructor over dissatisfaction with team members. Others have commented in response to the survey question, "Were you happy working in groups on your field project?"

▲ We all had very different personalities and conflicted a lot. Writing styles were different, but most of us just dealt with it.

▲ It was nice to work in groups, but as always, there was more cooperation from some members than others.

To partially alleviate the problem of group incompatibility, students are given the option to generate an individual paper (based on group-collected data), providing they declare a wish to do so by a predetermined date midway through the semester. Few students have used this option; most seem to prefer to work out any difficulties in their groups.

Field projects require more schedule flexibility on the part of students than would a traditional lab format. Although the minimum time commitment required is only 26 hours, many students choose to spend more time. In addition, field work does not lend itself to set two-hours-per-week scheduling because of the vagaries of weather and because many experiments require more intense work at particular times

Table 2. *An example of a field study in Ecology (single hypothesis and prediction).*

General Context: The top-down trophic cascade model (Hairston, Smith, Slobodkin 1960) holds that herbivore abundance tends to be limited by predators. The model predicts that predator removal should allow herbivores to increase and depress abundance of primary producers.

Tractable ecological question: Do effects of predation on herbivores affect algal abundance in aquatic ecosystems?

Hypothesis/prediction: The presence of aquatic predators on herbivores controls the abundance of algae in a pond. The elimination of predators results in increased algal growth. To test the prediction, students constructed herbivore and predator enclosures in a small eutrophic pond. They compared the growth of producers (algae) with and without the exclusion of herbivores (snails) and predators (fish).

Methods: Microscope slides were mounted on bricks (as a substrate for algal growth). There were three treatments: bricks enclosed in fine wire mesh to exclude snails, bricks in a coarse mesh to exclude fish but not snails, and bricks left open to the surroundings. Three replicates of each treatment were submerged at uniform depths near the north edge of the pond in early fall. Fish and snail censuses were conducted periodically. In early November, slides were retrieved and placed in known volumes of 95% ethanol. One week later the ethanol solutions were analyzed using a spectrometer to determine chlorophyll levels based upon absorbance at 410nm. In order to compare the mean absorbance of each cage to the control, t-tests were performed. (With three treatments, a one-way analysis of variance is a more appropriate statistical approach. Because many students have not had a statistics course, we prefer to have them use attainable methods that illustrate the philosophy and methods of statistical analysis, and we do not insist on the use of more advanced techniques.) Fish and snail census data complemented the algal growth results.

Equipment: Nine bricks, 18 glass slides, 4' length of chicken wire, 4' length of window screen, one spool of fishing line, fluorescent flagging tape, waterproof marking pen, access to visible light spectrophotometer for one 2-hour session near the end of semester.

Schedule:
• September 7: Identification of topic, operational hypotheses, experimental strategy
• September 14, 15: build and install experimental apparatus
• September through October: (each week) fish and snail census, monitor apparatus, conduct literature search, meet with instructors as needed
• November: remove apparatus, quantify algal growth, tabulate data, conduct statistics, generate paper (with assistance of instructor)
• December: submit work

of the season. Students have commented on the surveys that scheduling presents a challenge.

▲ Trying to organize around people's schedules was difficult, but overall there

were no problems.

▲ Getting everyone's schedules to coordinate was sometimes difficult.

In some cases, independent scheduling of the field lab can be an advan-

Table 3. *An example of a field study in Animal Behavior (multiple hypotheses, multiple predictions).*

General Context: Behavioral pattern: American Crows roost in large flocks in cities during the nonbreeding season (September through March). Crows arrive at roost trees at dusk, and leave to feed up to five miles away in countryside at dawn. Are there benefits that balance assumed energy and predation exposure costs of diurnal migration?

Tractable behavioral question: "What is the cause(s) of diurnal migration in nonbreeding American Crows (*Corvus brachyrhynchos*)?"

Hypotheses/predictions: (1) Predation hypothesis: Urban roosting allows escape from nocturnal predators (e.g., the Great-horned Owl [*Bubo virginianus*]); (2) Roost microenvironment hypothesis: Urban roosting reduces metabolic costs if city sites have higher night temperatures and lower winds than country sites. These hypotheses make different sets of predictions that do not overlap. The predation, but not the roost microenvironment hypothesis, predicts that predators are more common in the country than in the city. The roost microenvironment hypothesis, but not the predation hypothesis, predicts (a) that windspeed is higher or temperature lower in country than in city, and (b) that crows will choose roost trees with low windspeeds high temperatures, and will avoid high winds at the tops of trees.

Methods: Roost trees are located and temperature, windspeed, and owl abundance are determined in both the city and surrounding countryside. Owl abundance is determined via censusing by playing an owl hoot tape in both areas.

Equipment: A thermometer, anemometer (can be homemade by students), tape recorder (can be in a privately-owned vehicle), and owl hoot tape.

tage. It allows for more flexibility in the scheduling of other courses than would a traditional block of time devoted to lab.

Instructors are challenged in novel ways as compared to more traditional lab implementation. For example, with no "recipe book" for the field projects, early stages of development require flexibility, imagination, and creativity as students are guided toward tractable experiments that do not require extensive equipment or exhaustive protocol. Thorough familiarity with the topics of investigation is mandatory.

Instructor commitment is light in mid-semester, but heavy at the front and ends of the field projects when getting students off to a good start and evaluating final projects, respectively,

require significant investment of time. More specifically, total time commitment is no greater and perhaps less overall than more traditional lab or discussion sessions—instructors hold scheduled discussion times and office hours and avail themselves by appointment. There have been no significant problems with excessive numbers of students seeking help simultaneously as a result of the drop-in discussion option.

CONCLUSION

When students are provided the opportunity to conduct relevant and extended field and laboratory work, they gain three durable benefits:
▲ they know they have made a small contribution to the field about how nature works,

▲ they gain an appreciation for the methodology of science (potential and limitations), and
▲ most importantly, they gain personal insights that make them more productive citizens whether or not they pursue the sciences as a career.

The attributes promoted through laboratory investigation—problem solving skills, critical analysis, synthesis of divergent information, willingness to take intellectual risk, drive for precision, creativity, and consensus building, to name a few—are far too important to reserve for only the select few in the advanced stages of scientific career preparation.

Undergraduate semester-length field projects like those that supplement Animal Behavior and Ecology at The University of Iowa can make major contributions to educators' efforts to build a science and technology-literate society. ❑

References
Bybee, Rodger W. 1993. *Reforming Science Education.* New York: Columbia University, Teachers College Press
Horgan, John. 1996. *The End of Science.* New York: Broadway Books.
Lazarowitz, Reuven, and Pinchas Tamir. 1994. Research on using laboratory instruction in science. In *Handbook of Research on Science Teaching*, ed. Dorothy L. Gabel. New York: Macmillan Publishing.
Merriam, Robert W. 1988. A function in trouble: Undergraduate Science Teaching in research universities. *Journal of College Science Teaching* 18(2): 102-106.
Moore, Randy. 1996. Hands-off science. *The American Biology Teacher* 58 (7): 387.
National Science Board (NSB) Task Committee on Undergraduate Science and Engineering Education. 1986. *Undergraduate Science, Mathematics, and Engineering Education.* Washington, D.C.: National Science Board.
National Science Foundation (NSF) Directorate for Education and Human Resources. 1996. *Shaping the Future: New Expectations for Undergraduate Education in Science, Mathematics, Engineering, and Technology.* Washington, D.C.: NSF 96-139.
Rhoton, Jack, and Patricia Bowers, eds. 1996. *Issues in Science Education.* Arlington, Va.: National Science Teachers Association.
Rutherford, James F., and Andrew Ahlgren. 1990. *Science For All Americans.* New York: Oxford University Press.
Sundberg, Marshall D., and Joseph E. Armstrong. 1993. The status of laboratory instruction for introductory biology in U.S. universities. *The American Biology Teacher* 55(3): 144-146.
Thornton, J. W. 1971. *The Laboratory: A Place to Investigate.* Washington, D.C.: American Institute of Biological Sciences.

Full Application of the Scientific Method in an Undergraduate Teaching Laboratory

A Reality-Based Approach to Experiential Student-Directed Instruction

Alan R. Harker

Classroom experiments are often designed for convenience, ignoring fundamental scientific processes. Even "hands-on" experiences seldom allow the student to define the problem or design the experiment. The example outlined here incorporates the entire scientific method in an undergraduate laboratory. The students were responsible for the entire process of characterizing a bacterium capable of degrading a chemical of environmental significance.

I must confess with some embarrassment that after 21 years of research experience and over 10 years of teaching at the university level, I have no formal training in one particular area of my chosen discipline. I have an advantage over many of my colleagues, however, in that I fully recognize my deficiency.

I have never been exposed to nor required to learn those theories or practices which surely must become second nature to anyone formally schooled in the art of education. I am aware that favored modalities and fashionable jargon change over time, but

the fundamentals of excellent teaching must remain fairly constant.

With the exception of those principles that I have acquired through hard experience, I am unschooled. Although I am considered by most to be a good and conscientious teacher, I have had the unnerving feeling for most of my career that I am constantly reinventing the wheel.

The gap between my training for my role as teacher and researcher is understandable and all too common. The focus of my entire doctoral and postdoctoral training was directed toward the production of significant research of publishable quality. I was offered my first faculty appointment largely on my record of publications. That record held out the promise of generating similar future results with concomitant grant funding and accolades within the scientific community. I was asked to give a seminar and judged on my ability to communicate, but my skills as a teacher were clearly of secondary import. I have served on a sufficient number of search committees to know that my personal experience is not unique.

This gap between teaching and research is not solely confined to faculty at large research institutions. Admitting that there are excellent teachers at all levels of education, it is still far too common to find teachers who cannot effect a synthesis between teaching and research. This problem manifests its extremes in elementary school teachers with math and science phobias and in university professors who cannot be bothered to improve their teaching skills.

My own epiphany in this regard came as a new faculty member at Oklahoma State University. I was asked to teach both an undergraduate and a graduate class in microbial physiology. The undergraduate class was to have an associated laboratory section. The graduate course was to be a discussion/lecture.

As I prepared the undergraduate laboratory, I shunned what I

Alan R. Harker is a professor in the department of microbiology, Brigham Young University, P.O. Box 25108, Provo, UT 84602-5108; e-mail: alan_harker@byu.edu.

considered to be the cookbook manuals that were then available. I drew from my own research experience and formulated a number of short experiments that represented the current cutting-edge research in the field. The laboratory went smoothly and seemed to yield the desired results.

One year later, some of those same students were in the graduate-level class. In the course of our discussions, I asked them to recall certain experiments they had performed the year before. To my dismay not one of the students could recall, without extensive prompting on my part, what they had done, much less why they had done it. Upon extensive reflection it became apparent that in designing the classroom experiments I had ignored, for convenience sake, scientific principles that I had intuitively practiced in my own research. These same principles

The author, Prof. Harker, with two of his students in a microbiology lab. Prof. Harker gives his students the opportunity to participate in all aspects of the scientific process.

are those which make scientific research a vibrant and exciting part of my life.

For those who do research the scientific method is an ever-present reality. It is so frequently practiced that we scarcely give its separate principles significant thought. When it comes to teaching, however, we ignore some of its most basic tenets. The scientific method may be stated in a number of different ways, but the basics include the following:

▲ 1. *Identify a problem or question to be addressed.*
▲ 2. *Formulate a testable hypothesis.*
▲ 3. *Design an experiment to test the hypothesis.*
▲ 4. *Perform the experiment with proper controls, several times.*
▲ 5. *Collect and analyze the data.*
▲ 6. a. *If the confirmed data fail to support the hypothesis return to and formulate a new hypothesis and experimental protocol.*
   b. *If the confirmed data support the hypothesis report the findings of the experiment.*

Even in "hands-on" experiences, most instructional laboratories incorporate only steps 4, 5, and 6b. We seldom allow the student to design the experiment, much less define the problem. Step 6a is naturally obviated because we design laboratory exercises that cannot fail to yield the desired results.

If, as teachers, we fail to give our students the opportunity to participate in all portions of the real scientific process, we are depriving them of the excitement of science, of experiences that reinforce concepts, of the ability to learn through multiple means and senses. Hands-on experiences are little better than book learning if the students report their findings on fill-in-the-blank forms, or if we do not allow

them sufficient flexibility in the formulation of the problem.

Full participation in each step of the scientific method gives the student interest and ownership in the process of science regardless of the outcome. The example that follows is my attempt to incorporate the entire scientific method into an undergraduate course in microbial physiology.

COURSE DESIGN

The issue to be addressed in the laboratory was drawn from my own research interest, which is the application of bacterial metabolism to the degradation of environmental pollutants (bioremediation). The students were expected to describe, as completely as possible, a bacterium or a consortium of bacteria that is capable of degrading a chemical compound of some environmental significance.

Each research project was to be submitted first as a short proposal. The only stipulations were that: 1) the students justify the importance of investigating a particular compound, 2) the compound not be so toxic as to cause undue concern to the university safety committee or those involved in the experiment, and 3) there be a published assay that could be used to identify the presence or disappearance of the compound.

These simple requirements necessitated some library research on the part of the students. They familiarized themselves with the environmental literature, bulletins from the Environmental Protection Agency, and Material Safety Data Sheets (MSDS) classifications. The students were allowed to work alone or in groups no larger than three. Science is inherently a collaborative endeavor. Most of the students recognized the utility of such relationships and chose to work in small groups.

Every effort was made to stress the importance of the process over the end result. The recognition that each project was unique brought a realization that each was going to experience unique difficulties and challenges. Each would progress at a different rate and probably in different directions. A few students immediately dropped the class in deference to their GPA, despite my attempts to convince the students that their grade would depend on the quality of their work and not their progress relative to other groups.

The general rule of the class was that each group was entirely responsible for its own project. This included everything from making their own solutions and media to cleaning glassware. My responsibility was to ensure that all of the necessary supplies, instruments, and items of equipment were made available in a timely manner.

The laboratory class was scheduled to meet on a regular basis. In practice, much of what was accomplished occurred outside of those regular hours. Every other week one of our classroom periods was dedicated to the "lab meeting." Each group gave a short presentation on its project, allowing time for questions and comment from the rest of the class.

The tenor of these meetings was not one of completion or success, but usually one of frustration. The students felt free to air the project's problems and difficulties without any stigma of failure being attached. The laboratory meeting became a time for other students to offer suggestions and participate in the synthesis of solutions to real problems. It was likewise a time for me to instruct them in areas pertinent to the course content.

The final objective of the work completed over the course of the semester was to present the project results both in written format and as a seminar. The written reports were to be the work of the individual while the seminar was a group effort. The written reports were required to be in a style and format dictated by any scientific journal. The choice of journal was left to the student, but careful ad-

herence to the style manual was required. The seminars were all given on a specific day, with public announcement of the seminar times and content.

It was recommended to the students that they treat this as any seminar they might give at a national meeting or for a job interview. This meant appropriate dress, formality in presentation, and proper introductions. One student took this beyond my initial expectations by providing the post-seminar refreshments.

STUDENT ACCOMPLISHMENT

The projects fell generally into three categories based on the types of compounds. These were fuels, pesticides/herbicides, and solvents. By the end of the semester most groups had isolated and characterized the bacteria involved. Some groups attempted assays of activity in whole cells and crude extracts in order to determine rates of reaction and simple kinetics.

The reaction of the students to the experience evolved over the course of the semester. The initial reaction was disbelief. Despite much effort on my part to convince the students of the utility and advantage of this approach, the novelty and apparently tenuous nature of the course caused almost 20 percent of the class to drop after the first meeting. The remainder, though willing to try, were clearly less than convinced. Most exhibited a distinct fear of beginning. Without explicit instructions they felt very uncomfortable

in how to initiate their efforts. I found juniors and seniors who were unable to calculate molarity or adjust the pH of a solution. The collaborative nature of the projects tended to buffer some of

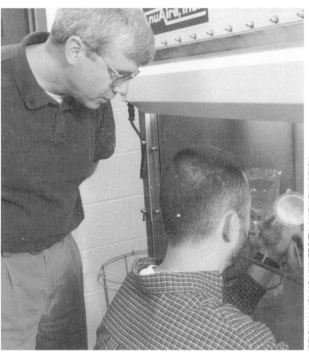

A student in Prof. Harker's class at Brigham Young working on the lab assignment: to describe a bacterium that is capable of degrading a chemical compound of environmental significance.

these problems as individual students emerged as leaders in their groups. A great deal of instruction was self-generated within the research groups.

After two weeks of feeling generally lost, there emerged an excitement that was palpable. Students began working in the laboratory at all hours. Visits to my office increased as well. Students were eager to show me their latest results, both successes and failures. As the students became more familiar with each other and their projects, the lab meetings became more productive and educational.

One particular group had initially produced good bacterial growth on their selective plates; but over the course of several weeks they were less and less successful in maintaining their culture. Discussion between students in the lab meeting revealed the difficulty. In an attempt to be more efficient, the group had made numerous selective plates at one time. The carbon source chosen, however, was fairly volatile. Over time, the concentration of carbon substrate decreased in the minimal medium leaving the bacteria nothing on which to feed.

The seminars given at the end of the semester were of a quality that indicated the student's personal engagement in the projects. Both the seminars and the written reports were well prepared. The quality and content were sufficient to judge the students' understanding of their projects and their relationship to the specific course content.

All of the students were interested in having their reports returned to them after grading. Since the class was taught during the spring semester, many provided me with self-addressed, stamped envelopes so that I could return the assignments. This is in contrast to many of my classes where a majority of writing assignments are never retrieved by the students.

I requested that the students write a short evaluation of the class. I hoped this would be more instructive than the standard bubble-sheet evaluation administered by the university. I was most struck by the comment of one student indicating that "this is the first original thing I have been asked to do in my four years at the university."

CONSIDERATIONS

The prospect of supervising a dozen research groups, all working on distinct and separate projects, was at first daunting. I was prepared to spend considerably more time than might be required to teach a more conventional laboratory class. In retrospect, however, the time demands of the class were not significantly different. How my time was allotted was merely different.

I had little time committed to class

preparation since the students were preparing all of the laboratory materials. My time was spent more in problem solving with the students and attempting to meet their resource needs as their research projects progressed. This was time spent more profitably than standard preparation time. I was involved directly with the students and able to teach more effectively because

For those who do research the scientific method is an ever-present reality. It is so frequently practiced that we scarcely give its separate principles significant thought. When it comes to teaching, however, we ignore some of its most basic tenets.

of that interaction.

A recurrent problem in this approach is the disparity in participation between the leaders that emerge within a research group and the student who is comfortable in the role of "wallflower." I found that this problem could be minimized in several ways. After the submission of the initial research proposal, I met with the individual research groups to discuss their projects. Part of this first meeting was a discussion of the division of labor and what was expected of each member of the team. I was very explicit that casual observers would not be tolerated any more than they would in a professional setting.

I required that the groups keep a standard laboratory notebook. Part of this book was to contain a work log. Each student logged hours in the labo-

ratory and the work accomplished. In each of the "laboratory meetings," a different student in each group was "randomly" requested to summarize the findings and plans of the group. This periodic responsibility ensured that each member of the group was intimately familiar with all aspects of his or her group effort and prepared to represent the group in the meeting.

Resources were at times a problem. The students have wonderful ideas that may not be practical because of the time or money involved in implementation. In my experience the students were amenable to discussing and implementing alternative approaches. The time spent discussing these alternatives allowed the "textbook" introduction to cutting-edge technology to be juxtaposed with more practical "bootstrap" solutions.

PERMUTATIONS

Although a fully equipped research laboratory would be ideal, such student-driven experiences can be managed successfully in a less resource-intensive environment. I have applied the principles learned in the physiology course to both ends of the spectrum: simple environmental problems addressed in summer camps for high school students and more complicated senior-level biotechnology classes requiring open access to the tools common to molecular biology.

The key to success in each case has been the design of the issue to be presented to the students. Inherent in that design are the limits within which the students are allowed to independently practice and apply the scientific method.
❑

Acknowledgment

The author's personal exploration of alternative approaches in instructional laboratories began during participation in a science education program at Oklahoma State University entitled Native Americans in Biological Sciences (NABS). The NABS program was generously funded by the Howard Hughes Medical Institute. He would like to acknowledge the support and encouragement of Dr. Robert Miller, department chair at the time, who wished to experiment with the departmental curriculum.

Student-Designed Physiology Laboratories

Creative Instructional Alternatives at a Resource-Poor New England University

Linda L. Tichenor

Resource–poor institutions could benefit by the use of student designed physiology laboratories and, at the same time, alter the way students think about how science is actually practiced. Given that traditional physiology laboratory manuals rely on the use of equipment and animals unavailable at some schools, different objectives for a physiology laboratory had to be developed for our university. The student-designed laboratories described here also addressed several recommendations outlined in various national reports to improve science teaching by providing a means of promoting higher-level thinking skills through scientific reasoning, analysis, and evaluation.

DEVELOPMENT OF COURSE OBJECTIVES

Response to Science Teaching Recommendations

The University of New England (UNE) is a private university in Biddeford, Maine, with a College of Arts and Sciences comprising, among other departments, the Department of Life Sciences. The department has a number of majors including medical biology, marine biology, and environmental science.

As the Department of Life Sciences

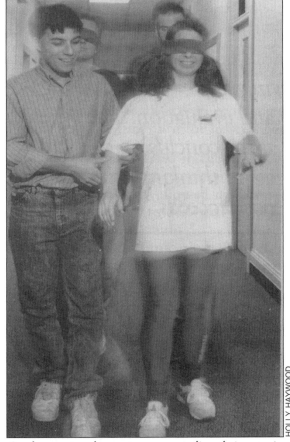

Figure 1.

Students enjoy the mystery surrounding their experiment. Two subjects are led from the hallway into the testing room.

HOLLY HAYWOOD

began to grow, curricular changes in the majors were being made. One such change involved developing a sophomore-level General Physiology course required of medical biology majors. Following departmental goals, the course was to reflect recommendations of several national reports that called for reform in college science teaching (Michael 1989; AAAS Report on the National Science Foundation Disciplinary Workshops on Undergraduate Education 1990; Moore 1993; Sigma Xi, 1990).

Concrete recommendations for improving college science teaching are found in objectives listed in the AAAS report on the liberal art of science (AAAS 1990).

These recommendations include:

▲ *engaging students in scientific investigation and scientific reasoning through goal-oriented instruction made explicit to the students.*

▲ *allowing students to discover the complexity of scientific knowledge through interpreting and evaluating data.*

Linda L. Tichenor is an assistant professor of life sciences, University of New England, Biddeford, ME 04005.

▲ *developing skills for finding, reading, and analyzing information by engaging students in scientific projects that require independent work and active learning.*
▲ *promoting the concept of the dependence of scientific enterprise on teamwork by creating problem-solving activities that include group research.*

All of these recommendations are oriented toward a student-centered approach, especially in developing cognitive skills conducive to the learning of science. Consequently, the recommendations became goals of the newly implemented General Physiology course.

Cost Efficiency
There were constraints imposed by

predesigned programs, nor were there physiographs and other classical data generating tools. There were no facilities to accommodate live animals nor were there plans to make provisions for them. It would be impossible to use typical laboratory manuals without using animals and with no equipment, given that most laboratory manuals written for physiology require using frogs for muscle/nerve laboratories, some type of amphibian or reptile heart to demonstrate cardiac regulation, and mice for endocrine physiology.

Since one of the goals of the course is to understand interrelationships and integration of body systems, we could easily use the human body as an animal model with little expense. A paper

Decreased Animal Use
The expressed mission of our university is to advance the quality of the human life and environment with programs focusing on health, the quality of life, and the environment. In the context of our institutional ethos, more and more life science students were challenging the use of animals in laboratories.

Moreover, several professional teachers' associations have advanced stricter rules on live animal use. In 1980, the National Association of Biology Teachers (NABT) issued a policy that did not allow vertebrate animals to be subjected to "pain or distinct discomfort" and in 1989 added to their policy the promotion of observational studies as well as support of alternatives to dissection and vivisection. In 1990, NABT stated that lab activities should not cause loss of an animal's life. Furthermore, no NABT awards would go to any project that harmed or killed animals (Orlans 1993). Also, the usual type of physiology laboratories in which animals are sacrificed had become an issue for many of our environmental science students who saw animal rights as an important environmental issue and called attention to the university's mission statement. Therefore, the new laboratory model reflected their philosophy, as well as the guidelines from national organizations and the university's mission statement.

The students thought and wrote about physiological mechanisms using student-designed laboratorics which provided a means of achieving higher level thinking skills through assimilation and evaluation. The type of discussion and analysis at the conclusion of each laboratory engaged students in thinking critically about how science proceeds.

---

our developing institution as our department attempted to respond to calls for improvement in the science curriculum using the guidelines set out by the national reports. The equipment available for performing physiology experiments was minimal because our institution, like many colleges, has been relatively resource poor. That is to say, the only equipment available were sphygmomanometers, stethoscopes, eyecharts, and a disparate collection of physical diagnostic tools such as reflex hammers and tuning forks.

Furthermore, the laboratories held no computers for generating data from

by Hansen and Roberts (1991) describes a medical physiology laboratory in which experiments requiring little capital expenditure were planned and carried out on humans. They suggested that this type of laboratory could be adapted for use in developing countries where medical schools are poorly funded. A live subject, one of the students, could be the source of data such as heart rate, blood pressure, temperature, fluid balance, ventilatory rate, and other variables. This model seemed appropriate for our institution, so I began to develop a similar program for the life science students at UNE.

Design as Pedagogy and Higher Level Thinking Skills
The Department of Life Sciences has been implementing teaching strategies that promote active learning (Tichenor and Kakareka 1995; Morgan et al. 1993). The General Professional Education of the Physician (GREP) report of the Association of American Medical Colleges (AAMC 1984) recommended that during baccalaureate preparation and preclinical years, faculty require students to de-

velop skills in problem solving as well as become active, independent learners. The new laboratory was to include pedagogy reflecting these current recommendations on engaging medical biology students in active learning.

Student-designed laboratories would be one way to promote active learning. Students would gain a better overall view of how science is actually done if they could participate in all steps of the process, especially asking questions, generating hypotheses, and designing laboratories to answer their questions. The techniques (i.e., laboratory skills such as animal surgery) that are learned in the classical physiology laboratory are important but so are the thinking skills involved in scientific enterprise. Therefore, the focus was placed on experimental design rather than technique.

According to the AAAS Report (1990), conventional science courses do not reflect the practice of science "at its best." The report recommends that laboratories should be open-ended and investigatory rather than confirmatory. Furthermore, the report recommends that the teaching of science should be driven by real problems rather than contrived textbook exercises and that pedagogical techniques should bring the spirit of scientific inquiry to undergraduate studies. Therefore, the idea of student-designed laboratories as part of course objectives became salient.

There have been several reports on student-designed laboratory experiments as an alternative to standard laboratory manuals (Stewart 1988; Mills 1981; Janners 1988). A student who simply follows instructions from a predesigned laboratory manual learns established principles or the details of techniques but will not learn about experimental design (Janners 1988). In such a laboratory, students do not learn to do science "as it is actually practiced," that is, proceeding from the inception of a question to experimental design to collection and analysis of

data. Stewart (1988) reported that in student-designed laboratories where students are allowed to plan their own investigations, they are more prepared

Figure 2.

Dr. Tichenor and her assistant remove the blindfolds from the subjects' eyes and make sure that the subjects are equidistant from the light source. Two students count the number of times that the subjects blink during light trials.

and are more interested in the results. She feels that students become critical thinkers when they are allowed to question how experiments are designed to determine "scientific truths."

Effective communication through writing is deemed as an essential part of scientific enterprise (AAAS 1990). Since teaching science as it is practiced must include how to write a scientific paper, weekly written assignments were used as a method of evaluating student progress. Each of these assignments was a portion of a scientific paper, such as an introduction, methods and materials, results, discussion, and a conclusion.

In summary, institutional constraints and agreed-upon academic objectives led to the following objectives for the General Physiology laboratory:
▲ To operate physiology laboratories with very little equipment available;

▲ To get students to ask and answer questions about interrelationships and integration of body systems by designing experiments generated from their own experiences, thus bringing the spirit of scientific inquiry (AAAS 1990) to answering questions;
▲ To promote critical thinking;
▲ To promote active learning and group research;
▲ To eliminate animal use from physiology laboratories;
▲ To develop scientific writing skills.

COURSE FORMAT AND PEDAGOGICAL ASSESSMENT

Using the resources that were available and the newly developed objectives, a pilot study was undertaken of the student-designed physiology laboratory model. During the first three weeks in the laboratory, the students formed experimental "teams," and each team would work together to design their own physiology experiment which would be used as a laboratory exercise later in the semester.

The first laboratory period introduced students to the idea of how experimental ideas come about. The notion that an idea could be sparked by communicating with other scientists or by looking at published work in refereed journals was discussed. The university librarians helped in the execution of the first laboratory.

The student "research" groups met in the library and became acquainted with the available physiology journals, since many of the students had never before consulted primary literature. The class became engaged in a type of "treasure hunt" as they searched for assigned topics in the literature. Part of the class assignment was to focus on the use of computer search lines as well as to peruse the physiology journals already available in the library.

During the next few laboratory periods the students practiced quantitative data collection by taking blood pressures under various conditions, recording body temperatures and reaction times according to exercises that I designed myself. Some tasks required that the students make observations of color change in peripheral skin circulation under various conditions, in order to give them experience collecting qualitative data as well. For the first few laboratory sessions simple questions such as "What is the effect of exercise on blood pressure?" engaged students in thinking about physiological mechanisms.

Students continued to meet in groups during and outside of the scheduled laboratory to refine their own experimental questions. Students were encouraged to ask their own scientific questions. As they soon discovered, asking good questions in physiological research was difficult to begin with and became more difficult when financial constraints had to be considered. As students began to submit proposals, small group conferences were scheduled with me to discuss the feasibility of their experimental design.

Statistical methodology was anticipated in advance and used to aid in the overall design, and controls were discussed. Each group had an opportunity to examine its question critically and to determine whether its experimental design would, in fact, answer that question. Because research groups were used, the students could see how science was practiced by a scientific "team."

The class would then perform the experiments with the students who created the exercise in charge of instructions and execution of the design. Given our small class sizes, there was enough time for each group to perform its experiment during the course of the semester, yielding six or seven student-designed laboratories.

Since one of the course objectives was to improve scientific writing skills, each week a writing assignment followed the laboratory. Instead of writing an entire laboratory report each week, students composed "parts" of a scientific paper.

For example, the first assignment was to write a literature review on the effect of exercise on blood pressure. The following week, the students wrote a methods and materials section on the effects of cold on peripheral circulation. The next week's assignment was to write a results section on that week's laboratory exercise. The experiment provided numerical data that could be analyzed, discussed, and written up in a results section of a scientific paper.

I evaluated and reviewed the writing with each student and allowed the student as many rewrites as possible until the paper was acceptable. In this way, the students practiced scientific writing in small, manageable tasks. One drawback to this type of evaluation was that it was time consuming for both student and instructor. However, students learned more about the actual process of writing than they would have if their work had been simply graded and handed back without the opportunity for redrafting.

For their laboratory final grade, the students chose their favorite student-designed laboratory exercise and wrote an entire research paper beginning with the literature review and ending with a discussion and conclusion. In addition, they were required to submit an abstract. They again had opportunity for rewriting their work at least one time. However, by that time, the students generally were well-versed on the details of writing a scientific paper, and needed only minor corrections.

The grading system was based on a point system which can be seen in **Table 1**. Because there were several opportunities for rewriting a draft, students usually scored 18-20 points on each assignment unless the student was less motivated to rewrite. The students would attach their rewrite along with their original drafts so that the instructor could determine improvement over time. Moreover, having all of the drafts together allowed the instructor to be more consistent in grading. *Writing Papers in the Biological Sciences,* by Victoria E. McMillan, was used as a reference text for style.

The weekly laboratory follow-up discussion provided a non-graded but valuable critique of the laboratory design. Since some experimental designs were naively flawed, analysis of design would generate lively discussions. **Table 2** demonstrates the typical type of questions asked to generate a follow-up discussion.

EXAMPLES OF LABORATORIES DESIGNED BY STUDENTS

One group tested effects of caffeine on manual dexterity and mental function. The experiment was performed on several students who used caffeine on a regular basis. The subjects were given increasing doses of caffeine (in the form of *No Doz* in amounts not to exceed their usual intake of coffee) and then asked to perform several tests.

One test examined reflex time as measured by distance a dropped ruler would travel before the subject could catch it with a finger pinch. Another test required the subjects to compute a series of mathematical problems in a given amount of time. Both accuracy and speed were calculated. Manual dexterity was determined by a sorting test. The subjects were tested for the amount of time it required them to sort a deck of shuffled cards into the four suits.

The following laboratory period was spent evaluating the experiment. The class generated discussion on controls, comparison of data among individuals, accuracy of scientific measurement, what could actually be inferred from the data, what was actually being tested, and physiological principles involved in caffeine effects on the body.

The second group tested the effects of extreme cold and extreme heat on blood pressure, heart rate, and body temperature in humans. Percent body fat was used as an additional variable in examining their data. The students arranged to use the walk-in freezer in the cafeteria as the cold chamber and the sauna in the student athletic center to test for extreme heat. The temperatures ranged from 4° to 110° F. Exposures lasted for a total of 20 minutes and recordings were made in five-minute intervals. Comparisons of responses were made between individuals with high and low body fat. The students did all the work themselves and organized the experimental sites, which required getting university approval, managing details of transporting experimental equipment, and organizing the groups into subjects and experimenters. The "researchers" arranged to have an exercise physiologist determine percent body fat on the subjects to compare with the other measurements. Again, an evaluation session was held during the subsequent laboratory period.

A third study group investigated a popular notion that blue eyes are more sensitive to light than brown eyes. After consulting the physics instructor, the students designed an apparatus that

Figure 3.

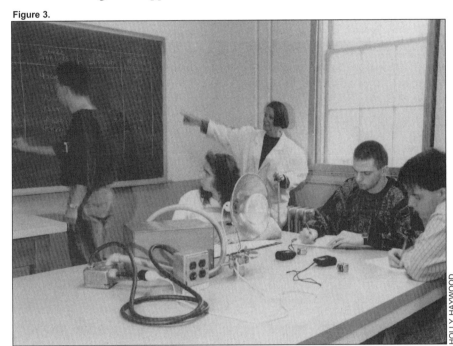

Data is collected and the experiment is analyzed for design flaws in a group discussion.

contained a calibrated rheostat for a 200-watt reflector lamp, which was used as the light source for the experiment. Numbers were marked on a dial and calibrated to varying light intensities in watts. Other equipment necessary for the experiment included stopwatches, blindfolds cut from soft cloth, hand counters, and meter sticks.

Subjects were blindfolded and placed in the hallway so that they would have no knowledge of the experimental procedure. (It was important that the subjects were kept uninformed as to the procedure.) After the procedure had been reviewed thoroughly by the "experimenters," two subjects were brought back into the laboratory and seated at the experimental station facing the reflector lamp. Measurements were taken to ensure that the subjects were seated equidistant from the light source. The sub-

jects' heads were positioned at approximately the same angle toward the light. (**See Fig. 1 and 2**).

Blindfolds were removed as the "ex-perimenters" began their observations. Subjects had been instructed to look directly into the light source without moving or talking. There was one observer who counted and recorded the number of times that the subject blinked during the trial.

The first trial began at 40 watts and lasted for one minute. The subjects were then reblindfolded for two minutes while the rheostat was adjusted to 60 watts. The second trial was repeated as the first. For each successive trial, the rheostat was increased by 20 watts until 120 watts was reached. One trial was performed in semi-darkness with the reflector lamp turned off to serve as a control.

After several groups of subjects had been tested in the same fashion, results were collated and displayed for the entire class to analyze. Following the collection of data, a follow-up discussion was led to critique the experimental design. The type of questions asked has been summarized in **Table 2**. Methods of analyzing the data were also discussed.

Figure 4.

Equipment is simple and affordable. A reflector lamp is connected to a calibrated rheostat device. Counters, stopwatches, and cloth blindfolds make up the remainder of the equipment.

STUDENT RESPONSE TO THE LABORATORY

There were some negative perceptions to student-centered learning. One major drawback is that of time organization. I had to evaluate written assignments within a short period of time. Therefore, I required ample time to work with students individually. Advising each group on experimental design several times requires a substantial amount of my time. As a result, scheduling conferences could be a problem both for students and myself who were often on different schedules.

Furthermore, problems arose if appointments were missed or had to be rescheduled in enough time to give feedback before the next writing assignment. Some students also perceived that the out of class meetings were a sign that the laboratory was time consuming and disorganized. If class did not fit into a tidy two-hour package, a few were negative towards the learning experience. An example can be seen in the following comment on the laboratory: "The class objectives were vague, and she seems to think we have five hours to spend on just physiology every night."

Objectives that include active learning sometimes provoked negative comments simply because some students did not like that style of learning. A comment follows that demonstrates how uncomfortable students become when there is no apparent "expert" defining laboratory procedure: "In lab, I think the self-teaching hindered me. We were doing labs that were supposed to demonstrate what we learned, but we didn't learn it until afterwards. I realize that this is how science works, but as demonstration labs, it would have been more helpful to me if I knew what was going on ahead of time." And, "Relies too much on student conducted classes and labs. We are not experts here."

Overall, feedback from the students indicated that the student-designed laboratories were more interesting than "cookbook" laboratories, and they felt adventurous in creating experiments. The students felt autonomous to a degree and were likely to be interested in questions they actually created for themselves. Students found that working on human subjects was more relative to their chosen careers in medicine and found that taking blood pressures and temperatures was more like the "real stuff." Some commented that learning to write scientific papers was the most beneficial portion of the course for them, and that science, discussion and "hands on" was the only way to learn. More often the comments were that labs were "fun and interesting."

The goal of eliminating the use of animals in this physiology laboratory seemed to draw favorable responses from students. A positive comment that reflects the nonanimal use in physiology was as follows: "Due to the controversy of animal experimentation here on campus, I am glad I got to experience a lab where students were the subjects." Traditional physiology laboratory courses use frogs, reptiles, and mice or perhaps even dogs. However, the students never requested that we shift the focus to include animal use.

CONCLUSION

The goals of group research and active learning were met through simple laboratories that the students designed for themselves to answer questions about which they are particularly curious. Students generate interesting ideas about physiology and often their naive notions have great potential for a teaching moment. Getting the students to participate in the scientific process by designing their own experiments proved to be a valuable experience for them.

In order to get the students to think and write about the physiological mechanisms, the student-designed laboratories provided a means of achieving higher level thinking skills through assimilation and evaluation. The type of discussion and analysis at the conclusion of each laboratory engaged students in thinking critically about how science proceeds. In addition, these dialogues were conducive to student learning about how body systems work together to sustain proper functioning.

Given the traditional laboratory manuals, the course had to be refocused on objectives that were different than mere demonstrations of physiological principles. The laboratories were performed with minimal equipment, yet addressed several objectives outlined in various national reports to improve science teaching. Thus, in a simple, student-designed laboratory, the principles of scientific questioning, experimental design, analysis, and evaluation are possible without the costs associated with more classical physiology laboratories. Resource-poor institutions could turn their attention to altering the way students think about how science is actually practiced by the use of student-designed laboratories. ❏

Table 1. Laboratory Grading System

Writing Assignment	Points
Introduction	20
Methods and Materials	20
Results	20
Results and Discussion	20
Conclusions and Abstract	20
Entire Scientific Paper Final	100
New Laboratory Design	20
Total	220

References

American Association for the Advancement of Science. 1990. *The Liberal Art of Science: Agenda for Action.* Washington, DC: AAAS Inc., publication no. 90-135.

Association of American Medical Colleges. 1984. *Physician for the Twenty-First Century, the GPEP Report.* Washington, DC: Association of American Medical Colleges.

Hansen, Penelope A., and K. B. Roberts. 1991. Human situations: a course introducing physiology to medical students. *American Journal of Physiology* 261:S7-S11

Janners, Martha Y. 1988. Inquiry, investigation, and communication in the student-directed laboratory. *Journal of College Science Teaching* 18(1):32-35.

McMillan, Victoria E. 1988. *Writing Papers in the Biological Sciences.* New York, NY: St. Martin Press, Inc.

Michael, Joel. 1989. An agenda for research on teaching of physiology. *American Journal of Physiology* 256: S14-S17.

Mills, V.M. The investigative laboratory in introductory biology courses: a practical approach. *The American Biology Teacher* 43: 346-67.

Moore, John, A. 1993. We need a revolution—teaching biology for twenty-first century. *Bioscience* 43(11): 782-786.

Morgan, Pamela, John Lemons, Jacques Carter, Owen Grumbling, and Eleanor Saboski. 1993. A scientific learning community at the University of New England: interdisciplinary approaches to introductory biology. *Journal of College Science Teaching* 22(3):171-177.

Orlans, Barbara. 1993. *In the Name of Science.* New York: Oxford University Press, Inc.

Stewart, Barbara Y. 1988. The surprise element of a student-designed laboratory experiment. *Journal of College Science Teaching* 17(4): 269-270.

Sigma Xi. 1990. *Entry Level Undergraduate Courses in Science, Mathematics, and Engineering: An Investment in Human Resources.* Research Triangle Park, NC: Sigma Xi.

Tichenor, Linda L. and Joseph Kakareka. 1995. An interdisciplinary teaching approach by integrating cell biology and biochemistry: a scientific learning community at the University of New England. *Journal of College Science Teaching* 25(2): 144-149.

Table 2. Discussion Following the Laboratory

1. How would you define light sensitivity? What do you think that the designers actually meant by the term, "light sensitivity?"

2. Do you feel that the experiment actually measured what it was designed to measure, i.e., "The Effect of Eye Color on Light Sensitivity"? Do you think that blinking is an actual measure of light sensitivity? Could there be other ways of assessing light sensitivity other than blinking? Did the results demonstrate increased blinking in lighter eyed subjects? (Surprisingly, most trials demonstrated that in fact, blue-eyed subjects do blink more than brown-eyed subjects!)

3. What other factors might cause blinking? How can the experimenters eliminate the extraneous variables and be sure that the blinking is only due to light intensity?

4. What other variables may affect the outcome of the experiment? (Long discussions usually ensue on caffeine intake, amount of sleep that subjects have gotten, nervousness during the experiment, laughing during the experiment, subjects' knowledge of what the experimenters are observing, and outside noises, to mention a few.) How can the experiment be altered the next time to eliminate extraneous variables? How will you talk about these variables in the discussion write-up?

5. By examining the data collected on the overhead, how would you best present it to demonstrate the differences between blue- and brown-eyed subjects? How do you present a set of data properly in a scientific paper?

6. What information should be included in the write-up of the results? What do you say about results in a write-up?

7. What information should be included in the discussion section of the report? How do you use literature to substantiate your results? Do your results and discussion, after careful scrutiny, support or refute the original hypothesis?

Problem-Based Learning in Physics: The Power of Students Teaching Students

Discovering the Interplay between Science and Today's World

Barbara J. Duch

One week you are a health care worker in the Winter Olympics at Lillehammer. The top French ski jumper has fallen and injured his hip. What do you tell him to do in order to minimize the forces on his sore hip?

Another week you are a traffic officer investigating an automobile accident involving personal injury. What measurements do you take, what data do you need to gather, and what assumptions do you need to make in order to discover which driver is at fault? How will you prove that you are right? You probably will be required to testify in court.

These are a few of the many roles played by students in my honors general physics course as they attempt to solve complex, real-world problems using physics principles. The problems

Barbara J. Duch is a teaching consultant in the center for teaching effectiveness, University of Delaware, Newark, DE 19716.

developed for this class demanded that students do several things: connect new knowledge to old; recognize what they know and understand (and what they don't); learn concepts thoroughly enough so they can explain them in their own words, and be able to teach them to their peers.

Many students dread taking the two-semester, algebra-based general physics course because they are not confident of their math and problem solving skills. Simultaneously, a large percentage of students (pre-med, pre-vet, and pre-physical therapy) who take this course feel pressured to get a high grade for professional school admission. Frequently, these students fail to see the connections between abstract physics principles and the knowledge that they need to succeed in their chosen careers. I designed an honors general physics course to demonstrate to students that physics is vital to their understanding of physiology, medicine, the human body, rehabilitation, and other health fields. At the same time, I needed to ensure that students

learned the traditional two-semester general physics curriculum.

In a traditional science class, learning tends to proceed from the abstract to the concrete, with concepts being introduced first, followed by an application problem. In problem-based learning (PBL), students are presented with an interesting, relevant problem "up front," so that they can experience for themselves the process of *doing* science: they proceed from the known to the unknown in order to understand the underlying abstract principles. Students who acquire scientific knowledge in the context in which it will be used are more likely to retain what they learned, and apply that knowledge appropriately (Albanese and Mitchell 1993; Boud and Felletti 1991).

Students worked in groups of four and learned to teach each other by effectively communicating what they knew—and what they didn't. They learned to depend on each other in order to successfully solve complex problems, and they learned to design and carry out open-ended experiments. Research has shown that students' achievement is enhanced when they work together in a cooperative learning environment (Johnson et al. 1991; Bonwell and Eisen 1991). Use of cooperative groups fosters the development of learning communities in the classroom, which reduces the high competitiveness and isolation of typical science courses (Tobias 1990, 1992; Project Kaleidoscope 1991).

In light of this research on learning, my objectives for developing this honors general physics course were to:

▲ Introduce physics principles through the use of complex "real world" problems in order to focus and motivate students.

▲ Emphasize open-ended experiments which the students themselves design.

▲ Require students to explain physics principles in their own words (in writing and orally) without equations, symbols, or formulae.

▲ Develop personal interactions and involvements among students through the use of permanent cooperative groups.

▲ Encourage students to "learn to learn" through a major research project related to physics and their career interests.

FEATURES OF THIS COURSE

The students in this course met twice weekly for 75 minutes and once a week for three hours. The three-hour session took the place of the traditional two-hour lab and one-hour recitation. The class meetings were all scheduled in a lab room with traditional lab tables. Experiments and field trips were generally scheduled in the three-hour time slot; however, discovery experiments were also planned during the 75-minute classes.

I selected a traditional algebra-based general physics textbook as the major resource for the class. However, I encouraged students to consult other texts, books, and articles. I did not as-

sign students the typical 10 to 20 end-of-chapter problems each week, since these problems tend to be narrowly focused and somewhat contrived. Instead, I gave students homework assignments of conceptual questions to

> *In problem-based learning, students are presented with an interesting, relevant problem "up front," so that they can experience for themselves the process of doing science: they proceed from the known to the unknown in order to understand the underlying abstract principles.*

answer at the end of each major topic. Many of these questions were taken from Arnold Arons' *A Guide to Introductory Physics Teaching,* Alan Van Heuvelen's *Physics: A General Introduction,* and Eric Mazur's *Conceptests.* These conceptual problems were assigned to individual students, and the homework was collected and graded. In addition, I designed more complex, "real-world" application problems which students solved in their groups each week.

I randomly assigned the 24 students to six permanent groups of four. Each individual in the group had specific responsibilities each week, with these roles (discussion leader, recorder, reporter, and accuracy coach) rotating regularly. Each group also established a set of ground rules and consequences under which the group functioned. Most groups adopted ground rules such as mandatory attendance at class and group meetings, advance preparation for class and group meetings, and a requirement that the reporter must show a rough draft of the problem or

lab one day before the assignment due date, among others. Students in their assigned groups worked through the real-world problems, connecting topics already learned to new ones, and teaching each other the physics prin-

ciples needed to understand the problem. Experiments were also designed to be conducted in groups of four, with each reporting on the results of their group's experimental conclusions.

There were two hour-long exams and a final exam. The hour exams and final exam had a group component (30 to 40 percent) which was completed before the individual part of the test. In some cases, the group portion of the test was a take-home problem, typical of the more complex, real-world problems given throughout the semester. The individual portion of the test consisted of the type of concpetual problems assigned for homework, and the more traditional end-of-chapter problems.

REAL-WORLD APPLICATIONS

Whenever possible, problems and experiments related the basic physics principles to the real world—especially biology, medicine, and the human body. In a traditional general physics course, students solve problems dealing with weights, bars, and pulleys in order to learn about the concepts of force and torque. In contrast, I challenged my students to use those concepts to determine how to minimize the forces on the injured hip of an Olympic ski jumper. They found that the forces were minimized if the skier's center of mass was shifted more directly over his injured hip.

Students in a traditional physics class learn to resolve vectors into their component parts and to apply equations of motion in two dimensions by solving end-of-chapter textbook problems. Students in my problem-based learning class used their understanding of these physics principles to predict the path of a basketball being shot by "Slam Dunk," a college player in the championship gme. Later in the problem, students were asked to calculate a force applied to the player's femur and predict whether the force was great enough to break the leg. They finally analyzed the resultant pulling force on the broken limb when it was immobilized using Russell traction.

Students in a traditional physics class learn about conservation of momentum by solving typical text problems involving colliding billliard balls and bullets fired into wooden blocks. Students in my problem-based learning class were challenged to use the principle of momentum, among other physics principles, to analyze an actual automobile accident. Given a description and sketch of an accident scene in a police report, they applied all the concepts they had previously learned in the course (kinematics, Newton's laws, work, energy, and momentum) to re-construct the sequence of the accident and decide which driver was at fault.

OPEN-ENDED EXPERIMENTS

The experimental investigations conducted by my students were open-ended and avoided "cookbook recipe" results. I asked students to design an experiment which would answer a

Students worked in groups of four and learned to teach each other by effectively communicating what they knew—and what they didn't. They learned to depend on each other in order to successfully solve complex problems, and they learned to design and carry out open-ended experiments.

question posed to them, identify sources of uncertainty in the data to be gathered, and plan ways to minimize that uncertainty. After they conducted their experiments, students were asked to explain reasons for any discrepancy in the results. For example, traditional classes measure moments of inertia of wheels, disks, and rods. I asked my students to estimate their own bodies' moments of inertia with their hands at their sides. (They approximated their bodies to be solid cylinders with the axis of rotation through the center, lengthwise.) They were then asked to predict whether the moment would be the same, greater, or less if their arms were extended.

The students then designed a way of measuring their own moment of inertia, in both positions, using turntables, pulleys, and weights. They compared their results to their predictions and explained the reasons for any differences.

FIELD TRIP EXPERIENCES

Students visited the University of Delaware Sports Science Laboratory several times during the year. They observed how force plates and computer analysis of the data of the muscle movement in children with cerebral palsy are used to advise doctors of the likely results of suggested surgical procedures. They also personally experienced stress testing with electrocardiograms (EKGs) and lung volume tests. They learned how to monitor and record their own EKGs and relate the graphs of EKGs to the physics principles involved. The University of Delaware physical therapy department faculty demonstrated many techniques used in rehabilitation which were connected to the physical concepts being studied. Students also visited the Medical Center of Delaware, audiology clinics, and various doctors' offices in association with medically related research projects, described below.

RESEARCH PROJECTS

In the spring semester, each group researched a topic related to their own career interests and the physics principles being studied. The research was conducted in and out of class, with students consulting experts (e.g., doctors, radiologists, and audiologists) on their projects. The groups were also expected to use a variety of sources for their research, including texts, journal articles, scientific and medical books, and popular science magazines. Each group made oral presentations to the class at the end of the semester based on their research papers.

Some of the topics chosen by the students over the past two years include:

▲ MRI as a Diagnostic Tool
▲ Uses of Ultrasound in Pregnancies
▲ Ultrasound in Physical Rehabilitation
▲ Electrophysiology of the Heart
▲ Surgical Corrections of Myopia
▲ Current and Future Medical Uses of Virtual Reality
▲ Hearing Loss and Hearing Aids

Students achieved a high level of understanding of the physics principles underlying many of these medical diagnostic techniques because of this semester-long learning experience.

STUDENT ATTITUDES

Student response to various aspects of this course on their final course rating forms was quite positive. When students were interviewed by an independent consultant, they all responded that working in groups aided their learning. Some typical comments from students on learning in groups were:

"Group work helped me see there's more than one way to approach a problem."

"The groups definitely help—not only if you don't know the answer, but if you have to explain it to others—you *really* have to understand it."

"Combined knowledge makes it easier to solve problems."

When responding to the question, "What did you learn that was new and meaningful to you," students answered:

"Physics is really, really important in medical issues. I never knew it explained so many things."

"I learned how much physiology depends on and can be explained by

physics. Also, physics is everywhere!"

"I hadn't realized how much physics actually affected the human body or how interesting it could be."

"I learned the beginnings of how to apply the knowledge that I learn in the classroom to real-life experiences. Too often, equations are learned, but two months later it is forgotten. This class left me with knowledge that hopefully I will retain forever."

Finally, students made the following comments about the use of complex real-world problems to initiate the learning of physics principles:

"They helped unite the concepts."

"They were intimidating at first, but once we got started, we realized how well we knew the material."

"They're like a mystery that needed to be figured out—so you wanted to finish it."

PERSONAL OBSERVATIONS

I was motivated to adopt this method of teaching because I strongly believe that students need to learn science as it is practiced. Students need to be actively involved in their learning, and need to learn physics in the context of real-world applications. With students working and learning together in groups, I found that attendance was almost 100 percent, and students were active, participating and questioning throughout class. Most incredibly, when coming for help during office hours, students had always made some sort of progress on the problem in question. I no longer heard students say, "I don't know how to start the problem." As the students themselves said, "Problem-solving (in groups) was less stressful, allowing for clearer thinking. Groups working together can usually solve anything—if they try hard enough." I think that the attitude toward problem-solving in groups positively affected the attitudes of the students as they did their individual problem-solving.

Would I return to lecturing in a tra-

ditional fashion? Not a chance. The excitement and energy of a room of students working in groups, teaching each other, challenging each other, and questioning each other is what I'll always want to see in my classroom.

Preliminary results indicate that active group learning and connections to real-world applications help students learn physics and apply that knowledge appropriately. Students state that they like the complex problems that interconnect the concepts. And doing problems in groups demonstrates vividly to students that there are many ways to solve a problem—not just one elusive strategy.

I believe that some of the important aspects of problem-based learning can be incorporated in large class settings. The complex real-world problems may need to be more structured, with guiding questions added. Incorporating some group activities with class discussion and lecture will allow students to have the structure and support necessary in large classes, while at the same time challenging and motivating them to really understand and enjoy physics. ❏

References
Albanese, M.A. and S. Mitchell. 1993. Problem-based learning: a review of literature on its outcomes and implementation issues. *Academic Medicine* 68: 52-81.
Aron, A.B. 1990. *A Guide to Introductory Physics Teaching.* New York: John Wiley and Sons.
Bonwell, C.C. and J.A. Eison. 1991. *Active learning: Creating excitement in the classroom.* ASHE-ERIC Higher Education Report No. 1. Washington, D.C.: George Washington University.
Boud, D. and G. Feletti, eds. 1991. *The challenge of problem-based learning in education for the professions.* Sydney, Australia: Herdsa.
Johnson, D.W., R.T. Johnson, and K.A. Smith. 1991. *Cooperative learning: Increasing college faculty instructional activity.* ASHE-ERIC Higher Education Report No. 4. Washington, D.C.: George Washington University.
Mazur, E. 1993. *Conceptests.* Cambridge, MA: Harvard University Press.
Project Kaleidoscope. 1991. *What works: Building natural science communities.* Volume One. Washington, D.C.: Stamats Communications, Inc.
Tobias, S. 1990. *They're not dumb, they're different.* Tucson, AZ: Research Corporation.
Tobias, S. 1992. *Revitalizing undergraduate science.* Tucson, AZ: Research Corporation.
Van Heuvelen, A. 1986. *Physics: a general introduction.* New York: Harper Collins.

A Multidimensional Approach to Teaching Biology

Injecting Analytical Thought into the Scientific Process

Dwight D. Dimaculangan, Paula L. Mitchell, William Rogers,
John M. Schmidt, Janice L. Chism, and James W. Johnston

This article describes a series of investigative courses that emphasize the process of science using original research projects. Each course is tailored to different types of students including biology majors, nonscience liberal arts majors, and early education majors. The overall course design can serve as a model for curriculum development.

In a collaborative effort among the biology faculty at Winthrop University in South Carolina, we developed three investigative courses that focus on the process of science using original research projects that students design, implement, analyze, and present in a scientific format. The courses are tailored to students with different levels of understanding of science including biology majors, nonscience liberal arts majors, and early education majors.

We are not alone in believing that students need to learn the methods and practices used by scientists. College science teachers increasingly recognize the importance of engaging undergraduates in research early in their

careers. For example, Keepers and Morier (1994) and Hobson (1996) outline courses that focus on the scientific method while Stager (1994), Stukus and Lennox (1995), Arce and Betancourt (1997), and Norton et al. (1997) describe the successful incorporation of research-based laboratories in introductory courses. More recently, Chaplin et al. (1998) presented their version of a research course: a four-week freshman course for majors entitled Introduction to Biological Research.

In this paper we describe a successful, well-tested, yet evolving set of courses that has become a central component of our curriculum and involves the majority of the faculty in the department. Our course design can serve as a model for other institutions trying to incorporate investigative courses on a large scale into their curricula.

COURSE DESIGN

In contrast to traditional content courses, the semester is dedicated to three main areas: 1) fundamentals of scientific method, hypothesis formation, and experimental design; 2) data collection, statistical analysis, and in-

terpretation of results; and 3) dissemination of scientific information through written and oral communication. Each instructor tailors the pace of each class and the course material to the specific student audience.

We teach the scientific method using a project-oriented approach. Students are expected to formulate questions and hypotheses, design experiments to test the hypotheses, develop quantitative skills, and reach appropriate conclusions. For example, the instructor and students discuss what constitutes a good hypothesis (i.e., one that is specific and testable) and how experiments should be designed to test one or more variables with measurable results.

Since it is closely associated with

Dwight D. Dimaculangan and John M. Schmidt are assistant professors, Paula L. Mitchell, William Rogers, and Janice L. Chism are associate professors, and James W. Johnston is a professor, department of biology, Winthrop University, Rock Hill, SC 29733; e-mail: dimaculangad@ winthrop.edu.

the analysis of data, we directly link statistical analysis with experimental design and data acquisition. Students learn the role of statistics and the requirements for choosing the correct tests. The central text for all three courses, *A Handbook of Biological Investigation,* by Ambrose and Ambrose (1995), introduces the concepts of data types and the scales on which data are measured as well as the statistical tests.

In the third skill area, the dissemination of scientific information, students write papers in the standard scientific format including an abstract, introduction, methods and materials, results, and discussion sections, and literature cited. They also report their findings to the other students through oral reports and a poster presentation at the end of the semester. In addition, students obtain background information on experimental topics using library and Internet resources. This lesson can include a class period at the library where a reference librarian introduces the resources that are currently available at our institution. We find that many students, especially nonscience majors, are unfamiliar with scientific references and databases.

COURSE PROGRESSION

Hypothesis formation, experimental design, statistical analysis, and scientific writing are interconnected in these courses through hands-on testing of ideas. Courses start with simple projects in which students work together to build basic skills, and end with students working individually on month-long projects. We find the steady progression from group learning to individual autonomy is an excellent way for students to master science.

The first few weeks of the semester, we mix lectures, class activities, and homework assignments. Lectures generally cover the scientific method, emphasizing the role of inductive and deductive reasoning, hypothesis formation and testing, Popper's ideas about the importance of falsification, and the concept of science as a cycle rather than as a linear progression toward ultimate truth. We introduce several statistical tests, and the students locate appropriate library resources.

During other class sessions, students work in groups of three or four and begin forming hypotheses to explain natural phenomena. They then make predictions based on each hypothesis and propose ways to test their predictions through observation or experiment. Brainstorming helps the students develop the critical-thinking skills necessary for scientific investigation. Indeed, the most daunting task is to teach students how to come up with an original idea that can be developed into a meaningful short-term experiment.

One initial exercise we often use is to have students write down a question that can be addressed using the scientific method. No other restrictions are given; in fact, they are encouraged to ask big questions. For example, in one class, a group of students produced the straightforward question, "Does the stitching pattern of a soccer ball affect its flight?" while another group thought of the more challenging question, "Do humans learn how to kiss?" Students then develop predictions based on various research hypotheses. In the latter example, some students predicted that if kissing is learned then this behavior may not be evident in all cultures, suggesting a natural experiment using observation alone.

The goal is to arrive at a research hypothesis that can be tested experimentally and completed at minimal cost within two to four weeks. We stress observation, hypothesis building, and experimental design along the way as necessary steps in obtaining unequivocal answers to questions. The entire procedure is repeated several times so that students gain confidence investigating questions that interest them.

Table 1. Mini-Investigation Exercises

Teaching Examples:
▲ Roll of die: Dice are rolled to see if each number comes up with equal frequency.

▲ Flip of coin: Coins are flipped to see if each face comes up with equal frequency.

Exercises:
▲ Insect color selection: Mealworms are placed on a color wheel to determine if they have color preferences.

▲ M&M™ Distribution: Bags of candy are used to determine if the actual color distribution is the same as the manufacturer's stated distribution.

▲ Zener cards: Zener cards (Rhine et al. 1940) are used to test for "psychic abilities" such as clairvoyance, telepathy, or precognition.

▲ Hexaflexagon: Paper polygons with different colored faces are constructed, and the likelihood of particular colors appearing when the polygon is flexed is determined. For folding technique, consult Gardner (1959).

▲ Student populations: Students compare the number of males and females using the library, the gym, and the cafeteria to their actual enrollments in the university.

▲ The Mini-Investigation: A Group Start

The first experiment is done as a class or with students working in groups of three to four members. In this exercise, referred to as a *mini-investigation,* the instructor provides a question on which to focus. Each group must form a hypothesis and design an experiment to test the vari-

Elementary education majors at Winthrop University in South Carolina investigating cricket behavior.

able of interest while trying to minimize confounding variables. The mini-investigation also introduces the use of statistics in data analysis and the art of scientific writing. Several simple, low cost, exercises are commonly used in our courses (**Table 1**) to demonstrate Chi square statistics, the first tests taught in the semester. The instructor allows the students to complete the investigation with as much independence as possible.

Finally, the students report their findings in a paper written in scientific format either as a group or as individuals. Each team member writes a specific part of the report (e.g., the abstract and introduction or the materials and methods), and is graded on his or her particular piece of the final

product. For subsequent group papers, responsibility for the various sections shifts in a round-robin fashion, so that students eventually receive feedback on all aspects of scientific writing. Each student's grade depends only on his or her specific contribution because that piece is graded independently of the others. Although these early assignments only constitute a minimal number of grade points, we give the students as much written feedback as possible and strongly recommend using them as guides for future writing assignments.

▲ The Team Investigation: Group Autonomy

After the mini-investigation, there follows a series of *team investigations* wherein the small student groups develop a question and a formal proposal in some area of biology determined by the instructor. Topics often include arthropod, annelid, fish, or human behavior, seed germination, and aerobic respiration. After a proposal is approved, each team works to test its hypotheses and answer its initial question.

The instructor gives minimal instruction on how to carry out the in-

vestigations. Our guiding principle is that doing science requires the exercise of imagination and the opportunity to make decisions, even poor ones. Students get better at doing research by experiencing both the positive and negative consequences of their decisions, including choices about sample size, sampling method, variables to be tested, and so on. Not all students welcome this autonomy, but working as part of a team initially helps them become comfortable with this new level of involvement and responsibility.

▲ The Independent Project

Students eventually plan and carry out an individual project, which comprises one fourth to one third of the final grade. Students are expected to be completely autonomous; they are personally responsible for the success of these individual projects. The project includes a formal proposal, a written report, an oral report to the class, and a poster presented at a public session attended by students in all of the investigative courses, departmental faculty, and the dean. We attempt to reproduce for students the experience of presenting research results at a scientific conference.

▲ Examinations

Although these courses are primarily investigative, testing is still an important component. There are usually two separate midterm examinations, one covering the philosophy and methods of science including definitions, explanations, and critical thinking, and another testing the students' mastery of statistics. In addition, instructors usually give a cumulative final. Our approach to testing statistics is very pragmatic: we have students select the appropriate statistical treatment for a particular question, and many of us give open book tests on the statistics part of the course.

GOOD SCIENCE WITH LIMITED RESOURCES

We believe that teaching the scientific method can be done without highly technical, expensive equipment. We argue, too, that such equipment can actually hinder teaching the basics of science since students could spend an enormous amount of time trying to master the technical aspects of the equipment without necessarily understanding the experimental design. Equipment can also limit the type of experiment to be designed and the number of students involved. Our courses emphasize the development of the fundamental skills needed for the process of science. Once mastered, students can apply these skills when working on research projects in higher level courses or on faculty-directed individual research projects.

We recommend students use organisms that are easy and inexpensive to maintain (e.g., arthropods, plants, seeds, worms, fish) and that experiments use basic scientific equipment including pH meters, light sensors, thermometers, and so forth. We encourage students to build any special devices from materials available in the lab or inexpensively purchased. Students can be surprisingly inventive under budgetary constraints, such as using cardboard tubes to create Y-tubes for insect or worm behavioral studies. Costs are also contained because the inclusion of the team projects in the course progression reduces the number of setups, and many team project systems are purposely inexpensive.

AN INVESTIGATIVE COURSE FOR NONSCIENCE MAJORS

Perhaps one of the most distinctive features of Winthrop's approach to teaching science is our interest in disseminating to nonmajors the methods, not just the facts, of science. To this end, in 1988 we and the physics/chemistry/geology department instituted a series of courses under the SCIENCE (SCIE) descriptor, SCIE 201 A,B,C,D. Each letter indicates a different branch of science: A - Biology, B - Chemistry, C - Physics, D - Geology. This discussion will be limited to the

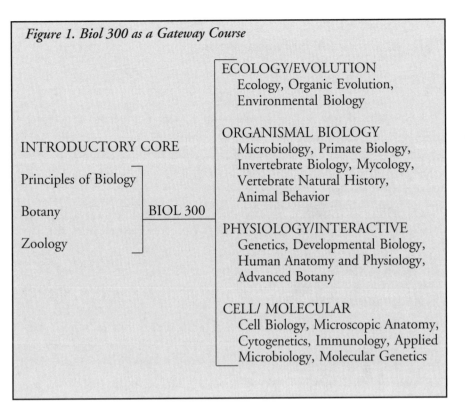

Figure 1. Biol 300 as a Gateway Course

INTRODUCTORY CORE

Principles of Biology

Botany

Zoology

BIOL 300

ECOLOGY/EVOLUTION
Ecology, Organic Evolution, Environmental Biology

ORGANISMAL BIOLOGY
Microbiology, Primate Biology, Invertebrate Biology, Mycology, Vertebrate Natural History, Animal Behavior

PHYSIOLOGY/INTERACTIVE
Genetics, Developmental Biology, Human Anatomy and Physiology, Advanced Botany

CELL/ MOLECULAR
Cell Biology, Microscopic Anatomy, Cytogenetics, Immunology, Applied Microbiology, Molecular Genetics

biology version.

Because the students in our course are often fearful of mathematics and science, we require them to master only three statistical tests: the Chi-squared test for appropriateness of fit, the Chi-squared test of independence, and the t-test. This reduces the likelihood of the students becoming too concerned about mathematics and forgetting that learning science is the main purpose of the course.

One common mini-investigation used in this class involves analyzing the distribution of colors in packages of M&Ms™ and comparing it with the company's stated color distribution. This exercise serves a range of purposes. First, it lets the students know that the methods of scientific inquiry can be applied to a variety of areas that students often don't think of as "science." It reminds them that sometimes mundane objects and observations about them can lead to interesting questions. It gives them more practice with hypothesis-testing and statistical analysis, and gets across ideas about experimental design.

For example, we have each student

first analyze his or her own M&Ms™ package and then compare those varied outcomes with one based on a pooled sample of many packages. Here we stress the importance of large samples and accurate sampling methods.

The students then answer biological questions with the team and individual investigations, as discussed above. However, we usually allow some flexibility with the topics for the individual projects of the nonmajors so that we can impress the notion that science and its methods can be applied to many supposedly "nonscientific" endeavors. Although most students investigate biological topics, they can choose individual projects in their own majors, in hobby areas, or based on their work situations.

For example, in one section, an English major tested whether the Cavalier poets really used alliteration statistically more often than did the Romantic poets. History majors have looked at questions such as per capita expenditures in social spending and their changes over time. We have seen a varied range of topics, but each requires critical thinking because

Table 2. Assessment Instrument Content

1. Definitions of scientific terms (e.g., hypothesis, dependent variable).

2. Appropriate questions for science to attempt to answer (e.g., Which questions are appropriate: Do animals have souls? Does the number of petals affect a flower's likelihood of pollination?).

3. Experimental design. The student is given a general statement of a scientific question and chooses the best version of an experimental protocol while justifying not choosing each of three others.

4. Graphical presentation of results. The student chooses the most appropriate graphical presentation and must justify rejecting each of three not chosen.

5. Choice of statistical analysis. The student is given a choice of statistical tests to analyze the data in Question 4 and must choose the best test while justifying rejection of the others.

6. Experimental hypothesis. The student reads an abstract from an investigation and must choose the statement that best describes the hypothesis being tested by the experiment. Rejections of options must be justified.

7. Sources of information. Students are asked to give, as specifically as possible, up to five written or electronic sources where they would expect to find relevant information on the experiment described in Question 6.

students must concentrate on experimental design instead of trying to master new jargon or foreign concepts.

INVESTIGATIVE BIOLOGY FOR ELEMENTARY EDUCATION MAJORS

Preservice teachers are offered a course called Investigative Biology, which was developed in 1980 at the request of the School of Education. It is the only course in biology required for the degree program in elementary or early childhood education. The topics assigned for the team projects (e.g., animal behavior, seed germination, leaf color and shape) teach students aspects of botany and zoology in the context of their research. We do not emphasize traditional didactic instruction, and we use lectures mainly to introduce the scientific method and basic statistical analysis.

The focus on biology is stronger than in the general education investigative course. For example, the students handle and maintain arthropods (crickets, mealworms, or pillbugs) and annelids, participate in at least one outdoor field collecting trip, and investigate a biological question through the individual research project.

The investigative design of this course is ideal since elementary teachers trained in science through traditional, didactic instruction techniques are less likely to feel comfortable teaching science. In fact, studies show innovative science curricula to be a more effective method of preparing preservice teachers than the traditional classroom lecture approach (Raizen and Michelsohn 1994). Furthermore, teachers who learned science through an investigative approach will be more likely to use this method in their own teaching, and thus more likely to encourage, rather than stifle, young children's natural curiosity.

TEACHING THE SCIENTIFIC METHOD TO BIOLOGY MAJORS

It was not until 1988 that a scientific methods course for biology majors

was added to our departmental offerings. Previously, our students were expected to learn about the methods and philosophy of science indirectly, in laboratory classes where traditional experiments were carried out, or by reading short introductory treatments in textbooks. The investigative course required for the biology major is called Scientific Process in Biology (BIOL 300), and it satisfies both a writing intensive and an oral communication intensive course requirement.

As a requirement for all advanced biology courses, BIOL 300 serves as a gateway into the major (**Figure 1**). Students can enroll in this course only if they have a 2.0 grade point average in the introductory core courses of the biology major plus one semester of chemistry, and have gotten at least a C in the required math and writing courses. We believe this grade requirement has helped ensure that the course is taken by better-prepared, committed biology majors at an appropriate point in their biology careers.

This course has had positive effects on other courses taught in the department. Increasingly, faculty have added projects based on original investigations to their advanced biology courses. These projects either supplement or replace traditional term papers and may generate posters that are included in the public poster sessions held at the end of each semester. Since most faculty teach one or more versions of the investigative courses, they have come to expect that their students are capable of carrying out such projects and to find that most students prefer them to library projects. At the other end of the curriculum, some faculty now introduce more instruction on the philosophy and methodology of science and an investigative component into their freshman biology courses.

ASSESSMENT

As part of a National Science Foundation-funded project, we have been engaged in an in-depth assessment of the effectiveness of the investigative courses. Here we provide an overview of some of our more obvious findings, based on comparisons of BIOL 300 and SCIE 201A.

All sections of investigative classes are given written pre- and postcourse assessments. The assessment covers seven skills (**Table 2**) and takes about 30 minutes to complete. Versions of the assessment for the majors and nonmajors are identical except for a slightly higher level of detail on questions concerning graphical (Q. 4) and statistical analysis (Q.5) for the former.

Results were compared using Chi-squared analysis (ProStat 1996) for three sections of nonmajors (n = 39) and five sections of biology majors (n = 61). Of the seven indicators studied, the most profound improvements were seen in the students' abilities to select the proper statistical test (1.2 fold increase for nonmajors and 8.9 fold increase for majors; **Figure 2A**) and in their knowledge of sources of information (2.3 fold increase for nonmajors and 1.6 fold increase for majors; **Figure 2B**). Results were statistically significant for both biology majors and nonmajors.

The two parameters that improved least were the students' abilities to select the proper experimental hypothesis (**Figure 2C**) and their mastery of appropriate applications of the scientific method (**Figure 2D**). In these areas we see no significant differences. However, since students typically come into the class with a good understanding of the concepts involved they have little room for improvement. For example, 72.5 percent of the nonmajors already understood the basics of an experimental hypothesis at the start of the course (Figure 2C). Therefore, the fact that the students did not significantly improve does not represent a failing in our approach.

FACULTY, DEPARTMENT, AND ADMINISTRATION COMMITMENT

We consistently offer several sections of all three investigative courses each year (BIOL 300, BIOL 210, and SCIE 201A) serving several hundred students. Nine professors in the biol-

Figure 2. Assessment of Student Learning by Biology Majors and Nonmajors

A. PROPER STATISTICAL TEST

$X^2 = 8.58$, df = 1, p = 0.0034

$X^2 = 46.07$, df = 1, p << 0.0001

B. SOURCES OF INFORMATION

$X^2 = 13.65$, df = 1, p = 0.0002

$X^2 = 19.14$, df = 1, p << 0.0001

C. EXPERIMENTAL HYPOTHESIS

$X^2 = 1.14$, df = 1, p = 0.284

$X^2 = 1.26$, df = 1, p = 0.262

D. APPROPRIATE USE OF SCIENCE

$X^2 = 0.003$, df = 1, p = 0.997

$X^2 = 0.009$, df = 1, p = 0.925

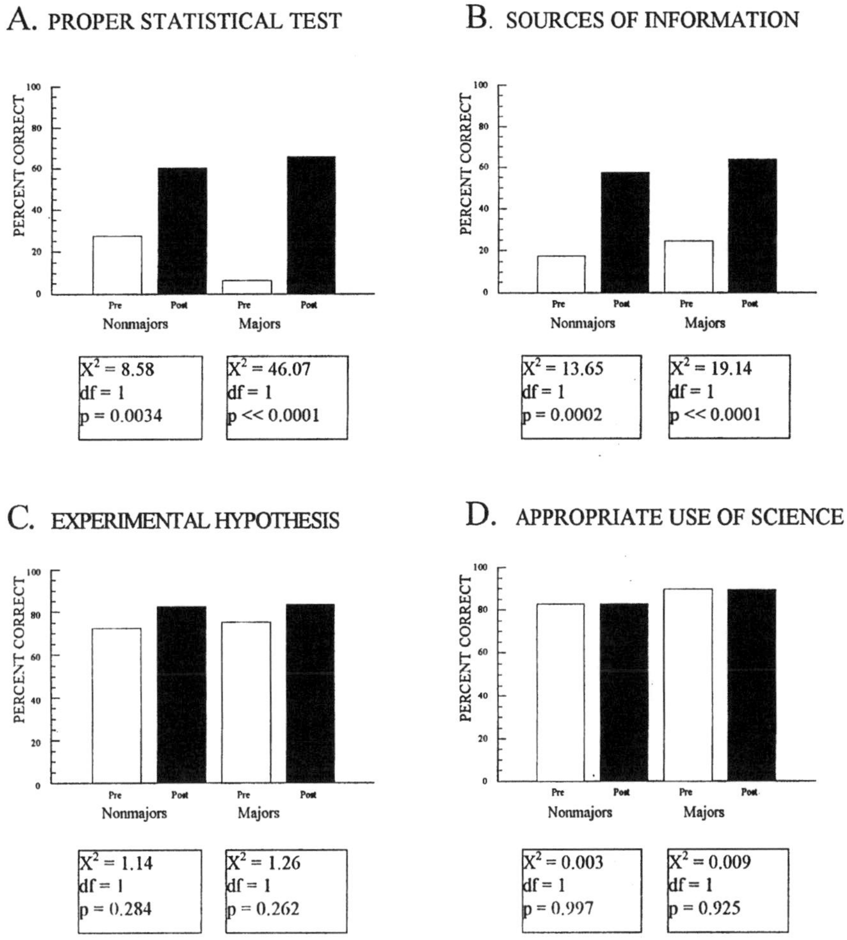

Statistical analysis was done using the numbers of correct and incorrect student responses. For clarity, the graphs show the percent correct for student responses.

ogy department (75 percent) regularly teach one or more of the investigative courses each year, resulting in a commitment of approximately 20 percent of our teaching load. This substantial commitment by the department would not be possible without the willingness of the faculty to teach these pedagogically difficult courses and the support of the administration.

The courses are a heavy workload for the instructors because of the required one-on-one interaction with the students and the grading of a large number of written assignments. We are now experimenting with using graduate students and upper-level undergraduate assistants to act as mentors

for needy students to help relieve some of the burden for the instructors. In addition, equipment must be collected, repaired, or monitored, and resources may be limited, especially during the latter part of the semester when the students are working on individual investigations.

Given the demands placed on the faculty, the administration can play an important role in the success of courses by keeping class sizes to minimum levels, supplying funds for equipment and supplies, and granting release time from teaching other courses. We find that the optimal number of students for each class to allow for maximum faculty-student contact is 16, but we often teach classes with 24 students.

Stumbling blocks can arise from a lack of cooperation within student groups, fear of mathematics, the responsibility of caring for living organisms, and time management. The instructor must be able to think on his or her feet and be prepared to solve a wide range of problems. The courses require experience and restraint on the part of teachers who must give guidance without offering specific instructions. Perhaps the greatest challenge of all for the students is the requirement of coming up with an original idea.

Still, most of us see, at least in some students, a dawning awareness that the world is a more understandable and predictable place if approached systematically. Some get truly enthusiastic about their projects and experience the rush that comes from discovery. We get a fair number of students who also realize that mathematics is a tool and not something to be inherently feared, and we find that these students really can use the techniques we offer to learn new things about themselves and their world.   ❑

Acknowledgments
The authors acknowledge with thanks biology department colleagues Dr. Richard Houk, Dr. Kenneth Gregg, and Dr. Julian Smith for their contributions to the investigative courses, Dr. Luckett Davis for his insightful review of this paper, and Dr. Roger Baumgarte in the psychology department who originally suggested the use of Zener cards to illustrate the Chi squared test. Determining the effectiveness of the investigative courses is part of a technology enhancement project at Winthrop that is partially supported by the National Science Foundation's Division of Undergraduate Education, grant DUE9650835.

References
Ambrose, H. W., and K. P. Ambrose. 1995. A *Handbook of Biological Investigation*. Knoxville, TN: Hunter Textbooks Inc..

Arce, J., and R. Betancourt. 1997. Student-designed experiments in scientific lab instruction. *Journal of College Science Teaching* 27(2): 114-118.

Chaplin, S. B., J. M. Manske, and J. L. Cruise. 1998. Introducing freshman to investigative research-a course for biology majors at Minnesota's University of St. Thomas: How "investigative labs" change the student from passive direction-follower to analytically critical thinker. *Journal of College Science Teaching* 27(5): 347-350.

Gardner, M. 1959. *The Scientific American Book of Mathematical Puzzles and Diversions.* New York, NY: Simon and Schuster.

Hobson, A. 1996. Incorporating scientific methodology into introductory science courses: experience and reason as guides to knowledge. *Journal of College Science Teaching* 25(5): 313-317.

Keeports, D., and D. Morier. 1994. Teaching the scientific method. *Journal of College Science Teaching* 24(1): 45-50.

Norton, C., L. H. Gildensoph, M. M. Phillips, D. D. Wygal, K. H. Olson, J. J. Pellegrini, and K. A. Tweeten. 1997. Reinvigorating introductory biology: A theme-based, investigative approach to teaching biology majors: Making science more meaningful at an all-women's college. *Journal of College Science Teaching* 27(2): 121-126.

ProStat. 1996. *User's Handbook.* Salt Lake City, UT: Poly Software International.

Raizen, S. A., and A. M. Michelsohn. 1994. *The Future of Science in Elementary Schools.* San Francisco, CA: Jossey-Bass, Inc.

Rhine, J. B., J. G. Pratt, B. M. Smith, C. E. Stuart, and J. A. Greenwood. 1940. *Extra-sensory Perception after Sixty Years.* New York, NY: Henry Holt and Co.

Stager, J. C. 1994. Just do it!: A research-based approach to introductory biology laboratory: Giving first-year students the opportunity for independent investigation. *Journal of College Science Teaching* 24(2): 91-93.

Stukus, P., and J. E. Lennox. 1995. Use of an investigative semester-length laboratory project in an introductory microbiology class. *Journal of College Science Teaching* 25(2): 135-139.

Authors' Affiliations and Contact Information

As of February 2001

Anton E. Lawson is a professor in the Department of Biology, Arizona State University, Tempe, AZ 85287-1501. e-mail: *anton.Lawson@asu.edu*

Deborah A. Tolman is a Ph.D. candidate in the Department of Geography and the Department of Environmental Sciences and Resources, Portland State University, Portland, OR 97207. e-mail: *psu03187@pdx.edu*

George E. Glasson is an associate professor of science education in the Department of Teaching and Learning, Virginia Tech, Blacksburg, VA 24061-0313. e-mail: *glassong@vt.edu*

Woodrow L. McKenzie is an assistant professor in the School of Education and Human Development, Lynchburg College, Lynchburg, VA 24501. e-mail: *McKenzie_W@mail.lynchburg.edu*

Philip Stukus is a professor of biology at Denison University, Granville, OH 43023. e-mail: *stukus@denison.edu*

John E. Lennox is a professor of microbiology at Penn State-Altoona, Altoona, PA 16603. e-mail: *jel5@psu.edu*

G. Douglas Crandall is a professor of biology, Emmanuel College, Boston, MA 02115. e-mail: *Crandall@emmanuel.edu*

Jeffrey D. Weld is an assistant professor of biology and science education at the University of Northern Iowa, Cedar Falls, IA 50614. e-mail: *jeff.weld@uni.edu*

Christopher M. Rogers is an assistant professor, Department of Biological Sciences, Wichita State University, Wichita, KS 667260. e-mail: *cmrogers@twsu.edu*

Stephen B. Heard is an assistant professor of ecology, University of Iowa, Iowa City, IA 52242. e-mail: *Stephen-heard@uiowa.edu*

Alan R. Harker is a professor in the Department of Microbiology, Brigham Young University, Provo, UT 84602-5108. e-mail: *alan_harker@byu.edu*

Linda L. Tichenor is an assistant professor of biological sciences, University of Arkansas, Fayetteville, AR 72701. e-mail: *tichenor@mail.uark.edu*

Barbara J. Duch is associate director of the Mathematics and Science Education Resource Center, University of Delaware, Newark, DE 19716. e-mail: *bduch@udel.edu*

Dwight D. Dimaculangan is an associate professor in the Department of Biology, Winthrop University, Rock Hill, SC 29733. e-mail: *dimaculangad@winthrop.edu*

Paula L. Mitchell is an associate professor in the Department of Biology, Winthrop University, Rock Hill, SC 29733. e-mail: *mitchellp@winthrop.edu*

William Rogers is an associate professor in the Department of Biology, Winthrop University, Rock Hill, SC 29733. e-mail: *rogersw@winthrop.edu*

John M. Schmidt is an assistant professor in the Department of Biology, Winthrop University, Rock Hill, SC 29733. e-mail: *schmidtj@winthrop.edu*

Janice L. Chism is an associate professor in the Department of Biology, Winthrop University, Rock Hill, SC 29733. e-mail: *chismj@winthrop.edu*

James W. Johnston is a professor in the Department of Biology, Winthrop University, Rock Hill, SC 29733. e-mail: *johnstonj@winthrop.edu*